LANGUAGE DEVELOPMENT THROUGH CONTENT
AMERICA: AFTER INDEPENDENCE

Anna Uhl Chamot

▲▼ Addison-Wesley Publishing Company

READING, MASSACHUSETTS • MENLO PARK, CALIFORNIA
DON MILLS, ONTARIO • WOKINGHAM, ENGLAND • AMSTERDAM
SYDNEY • SINGAPORE • TOKYO • MADRID • BOGOTA
SANTIAGO • SAN JUAN

A Publication of the World Language Division

Acknowledgments

Grateful acknowledgment is made to Lisa Küpper, Talbot Hamlin, and Elly Schottman for their contributions to this book.

Editorial: Elly Schottman, Talbot Hamlin

Production/Manufacturing: James W. Gibbons

Photo Research: Merle Sciacca

Design and Illustration: Bookwrights, Inc.

Maps: EX LIBRIS

Photographs courtesy of: p. 12, Federal Highway Administration; **p. 19,** Union Pacific Railroad Museum Collection; **p. 21,** Thomas Jefferson Memorial Foundation/Monticello; **p. 22,** National Cowboy Hall of Fame (ur), Oregon Department of Transportation (c); **p. 28,** California State Library; **p. 29,** Union Pacific Railroad Museum Collection; **p. 30,** California Farm Bureau Federation; **p. 35,** Woolaroc Museum; **p. 36,** American Museum of Natural History (ul), National Portrait Gallery (ur), (ll); **p. 40,** Texas Highway Magazine; **p. 46,** Cook Collection, Valentine Museum; **p. 51,** The New York Historical Society, New York City (l), Moorland-Spingarn Research Center, Howard University (r); **p. 53,** National Portrait Gallery (ur), Smith College, Sophia Smith Collection (lr); **p. 54,** The Metropolitan Museum of Art, Gift of Mr. and Mrs. Carl Stoeckel, 1897; **p. 62,** National Portrait Gallery; **p. 66,** Library of Congress; **p. 70, 71 (b),** National Portrait Gallery; **p. 71,** University of Tuskegee (t); **p. 72,** Brown Brothers (ur), National Museum of American History (ll); **p. 76,** Museum of American Textile History; **p. 80,** Lowell Historical Society (ul), California State Library (lr); **p. 82,** From the Collection of Henry Ford Museum and Greenfield Village; **p. 83,** Drake Well Museum; **p. 85,** Library of Congress; **p. 86,** National Park Service, Sagamore Hill Historical Site; **p. 87,** Stanley J. Morrow Collection, W.H. Over State Museum (ll), Union Pacific Railroad Museum Collection (ur); **p. 88,** Library of Congress (ll), Gail Zucker (ur); **p. 89,** Library of Congress; **p. 92,** U.S. Department of Agriculture; **p. 93,** National Air and Space Museum, Smithsonian Institution; **p. 94,** Lowell Historical Society (ur), University of Illinois, Chicago, Jane Addams Memorial Collection (ll); **p. 95,** George Meany Memorial Archives (c), Library of Congress (b), The Museum of the City of New York (ul), (ur); **p. 98,** New York Convention and Visitors Bureau; **p. 99,** California State Library (lr), U.S. Immigration Service (ul); **p. 100,** The Museum of the City of New York, (ur), Ralph P. Turcotte (ll).

ISBN 0-201-12930-2

19 20 - CRS - 02 01

To the Teacher

America: The Early Years and *America: After Independence* are specifically designed to help prepare limited English proficient students for curricular work in United States history and world geography. Through readings and language exercises, students learn the language of social studies and sharpen their reading comprehension. Through exercises based on maps, charts, and graphs, they acquire important interpretive social studies skills. Through listening exercises, they build both listening and note-taking skills. And through report development exercises, students gain combined practice in researching, writing, and speaking, together with further reinforcement in listening and note-taking.

The content core of the two worktexts is the story of the Americas, and particularly the part that became the United States. Interwoven with this historical survey is the study of geographic regions around the world. The two worktexts are transitional and preparatory material for mainstream classes; they are not intended as substitutes for social studies textbooks. Students who complete them will have acquired invaluable language experience in an academic context. In addition, they will have made a start toward gaining the conceptual background that mainstream young people bring to their social studies courses.

The worktexts present English language as it is used in the social studies content area. The exercises preceding and following the social studies readings develop academic language skills while reinforcing understanding of the content. A basic social studies vocabulary is built (see the Glossary at the end of this book), and a variety of learning strategies and reading skills are developed and practiced. Listening comprehension in the academic context is also emphasized. In each unit students listen to a "mini-lecture" and are guided through the skill of taking notes. The texts for these "mini-lectures" are provided in the Teacher's Guide. Many of the activities in the worktexts (and many of the suggested procedures in the accompanying Teacher's Guide) involve students working in pairs or small groups, giving them maximum opportunity to use language actively. Discussion questions, as well as a variety of other activities requiring social interaction, provide creative springboards for the development of thinking skills and oral language facility.

America: The Early Years and *America: After Independence* can be used effectively in both the ESOL classroom and the mainstream classroom. Instructions for the student activities are clear and complete. You will wish to go over them orally with the students, however, to make sure that each student understands what he or she is to do. In addition, the Teacher's Guide presents detailed suggestions for teaching each lesson. By following these suggestions, you will be providing your students with many opportunities to use their developing English skills. You will also be helping them to build a valuable inventory of learning strategies which will carry over directly into their mainstream work. One important suggestion concerns the assignment of students to pairs or groups. Mixed (heterogeneous) grouping is recommended wherever possible so that more proficient students can provide assistance and serve as models for those who are less proficient. The texts for the listening exercises are found in the Teacher's Guide only. You can either read these to the students or, if you prefer, tape record them for individual use. The Guide also includes suggested answers for all exercises in the worktexts.

America: The Early Years and *America: After Independence* are part of the *Language Development Through Content: Social Studies* series. This series aims to teach students the language and many of the skills they will need to study social studies subjects in the mainstream curriculum. At the same time, it helps these students to learn or review some of the basic facts and concepts presented in these subjects at the upper elementary and secondary levels. It can help your students achieve greater success in their mainstream classrooms.

Contents

*Teacher scripts are provided for these listening and note-taking activities in the Teacher's Guide.

Glossary

Index

Maps

*Teacher scripts are provided for these listening and note-taking activities in the Teacher's Guide.

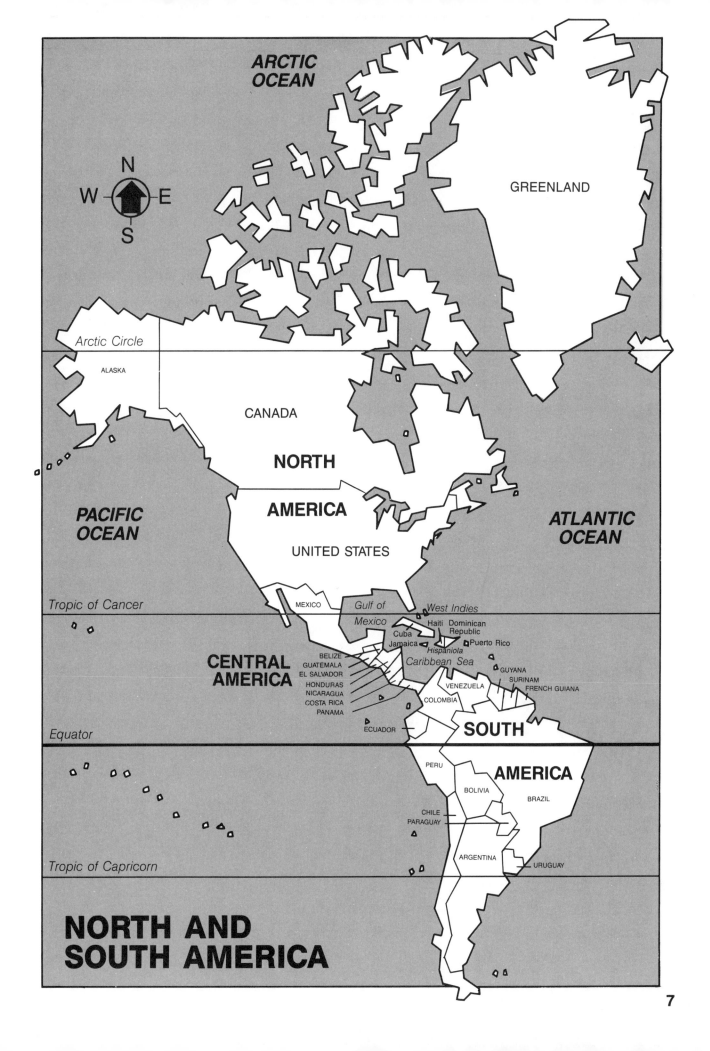

ARCTIC
OCEAN

N
W · E
S

GREENLAND

Arctic Circle

ALASKA

CANADA

NORTH

AMERICA

UNITED STATES

PACIFIC
OCEAN

ATLANTIC
OCEAN

Tropic of Cancer

MEXICO   Gulf of
Mexico   West Indies

Haiti   Dominican
Cuba   Republic
Jamaica   Puerto Rico
Hispaniola

BELIZE
GUATEMALA   Caribbean Sea
EL SALVADOR
CENTRAL   GUYANA
AMERICA HONDURAS   SURINAM
NICARAGUA   FRENCH GUIANA
COSTA RICA   VENEZUELA
PANAMA
COLOMBIA

Equator   ECUADOR

SOUTH

PERU   **AMERICA**

BOLIVIA   BRAZIL

CHILE
PARAGUAY

ARGENTINA   URUGUAY

Tropic of Capricorn

NORTH AND
SOUTH AMERICA

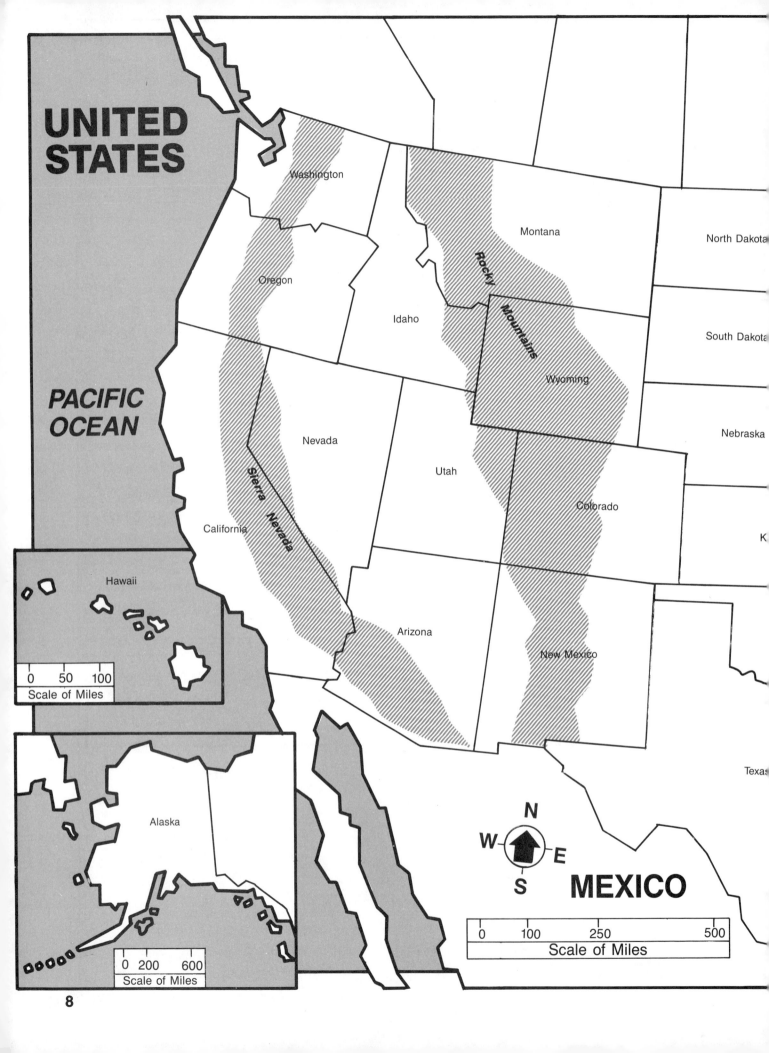

UNITED STATES

PACIFIC OCEAN

Washington

Oregon

Idaho

Montana

North Dakota

South Dakota

Wyoming

Rocky Mountains

Nevada

Utah

Nebraska

Sierra Nevada

California

Colorado

K

Hawaii

| 0 | 50 | 100 |
Scale of Miles

Arizona

New Mexico

Texas

Alaska

| 0 | 200 | 600 |
Scale of Miles

N
W E
S

MEXICO

| 0 | 100 | 250 | 500 |
Scale of Miles

8

CANADA

Minnesota

Michigan

Wisconsin

Michigan

Iowa

Illinois

Indiana

Ohio

Missouri

Kentucky

West
Virginia

Virginia

Maryland

Delaware

Pennsylvania

New Jersey

New York

Vermont

New Hampshire

Maine

Massachusetts

Con-
necticut

Rhode
Island

Hudson River

St. Lawrence River

Appalachian Mountains

Mississippi River

Tennessee

North
Carolina

South
Carolina

oma

Arkansas

Mississippi

Alabama

Georgia

Louisiana

Florida

Gulf of Mexico

ATLANTIC
OCEAN

Commonwealth of
Puerto Rico

0   50   100
Scale of Miles

WORLD REGIONS

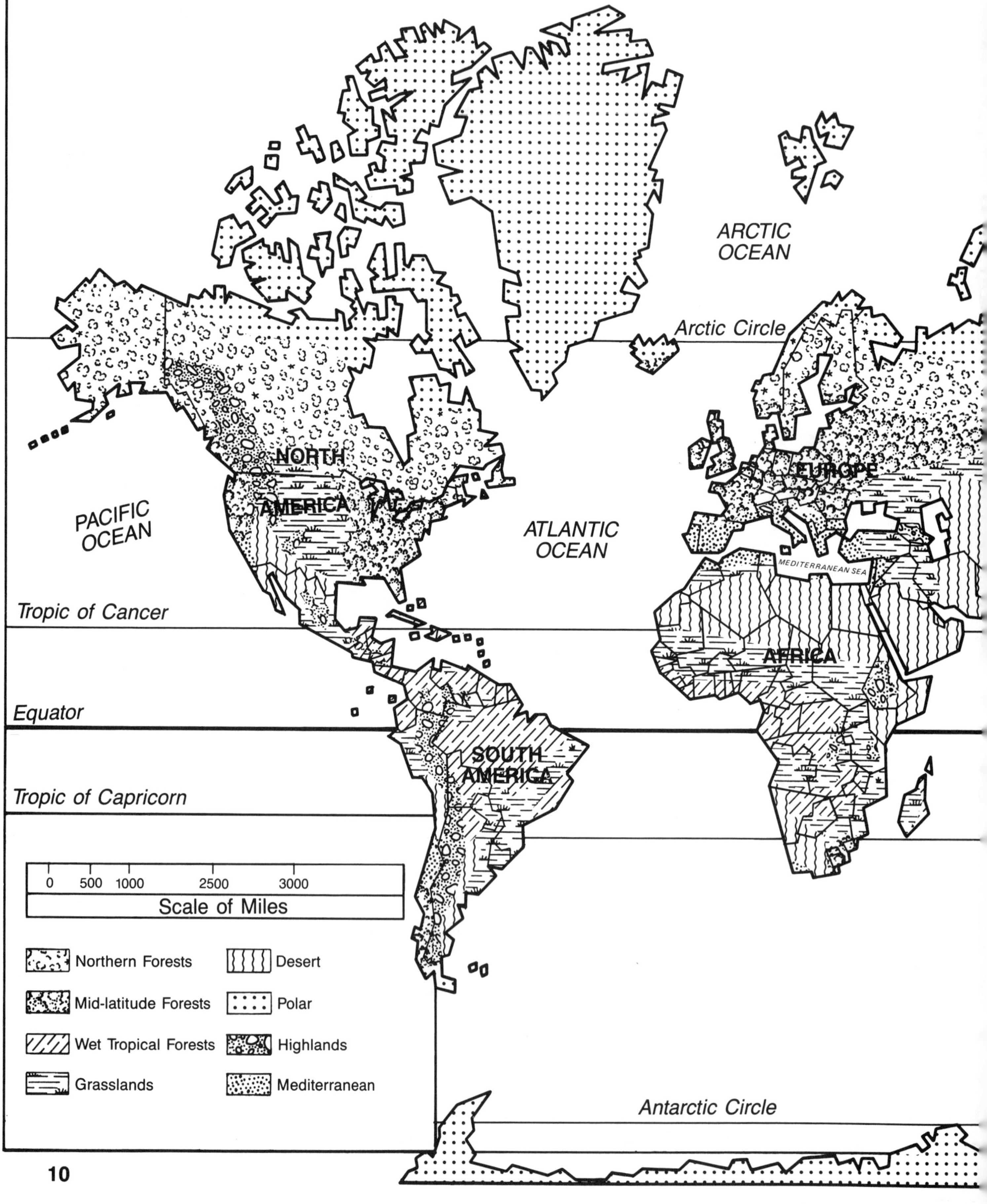

ARCTIC OCEAN

Arctic Circle

EUROPE

PACIFIC OCEAN

NORTH AMERICA

ATLANTIC OCEAN

MEDITERRANEAN SEA

AFRICA

Tropic of Cancer

Equator

SOUTH AMERICA

Tropic of Capricorn

0	500	1000	2500	3000

Scale of Miles

Northern Forests   Desert

Mid-latitude Forests   Polar

Wet Tropical Forests   Highlands

Grasslands   Mediterranean

Antarctic Circle

The Regions of the World

What Are Regions?

Regions are areas of the world that have similar climates, plant life, and animal life. The earth can be divided into many different regions. The map on these pages shows regions of the earth.

How Are Regions Different?

Some regions, such as the Polar Regions, are always cold. Some regions, such as the Wet Tropical Regions, are always warm. Other regions, such as the Mid-Latitude Forest Regions, are cold part of the year and warm other parts of the year. In the Desert Regions there is almost no rain. In the Wet Tropical Regions it rains almost every day.

People live in all the regions of the world. People in different regions usually live and work in different ways.

Using the Map Key

Look at the map and the key that shows the different regions. Find the United States on the map. The United States is a very big country. It has many of the world's regions in it. Find the following regions in the United States: the Highland Region, the Mediterranean Region, the Grassland Region, and the Desert Region. What is the name of the region you live in? Now look at the rest of the map. Where else in the world can you find the region in which you live?

The Nation Grows

In this unit you will:

- read about the westward movement of American pioneers
- learn about the new land that became part of the United States
- read about two important Presidents: Thomas Jefferson and Andrew Jackson
- learn about what happened to some Native American tribes in the 1800s
- learn about the Highland and Mediterranean Regions
- use maps, time lines, charts and graphs
- sharpen your listening, speaking, and note-taking skills
- do research and write a report

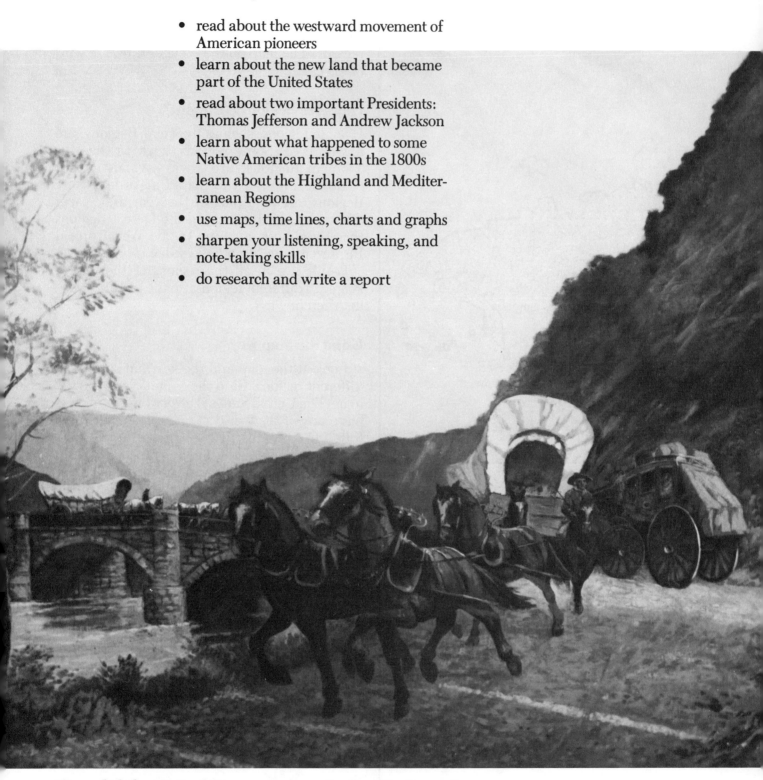

How did the United States grow to the Pacific Ocean?

Who explored the new territories?

Why did people move west?

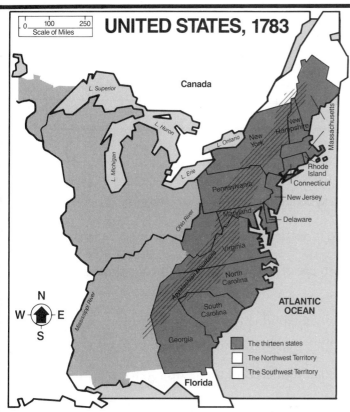

UNITED STATES, 1783

Scale of Miles
0 100 250

Canada

L. Superior

L. Huron

L. Michigan

L. Ontario

L. Erie

New Hampshire

New York

Massachusetts

Rhode Island

Connecticut

New Jersey

Pennsylvania

Maryland

Delaware

Ohio River

Virginia

Appalachian Mountains

North Carolina

South Carolina

ATLANTIC OCEAN

Mississippi River

Georgia

N W E S

Florida

- ■ The thirteen states
- □ The Northwest Territory
- □ The Southwest Territory

The United States developed from thirteen English colonies on the Atlantic coast of North America. The thirteen colonies declared their independence from England in 1776, but the War for Independence continued until 1781. England and the United States finally signed a peace treaty in 1783. In the next 70 years, the United States grew to the Pacific Ocean and the Gulf of Mexico. This unit tells about that growth.

This is what the United States looked like in 1783, at the end of the War for Independence.

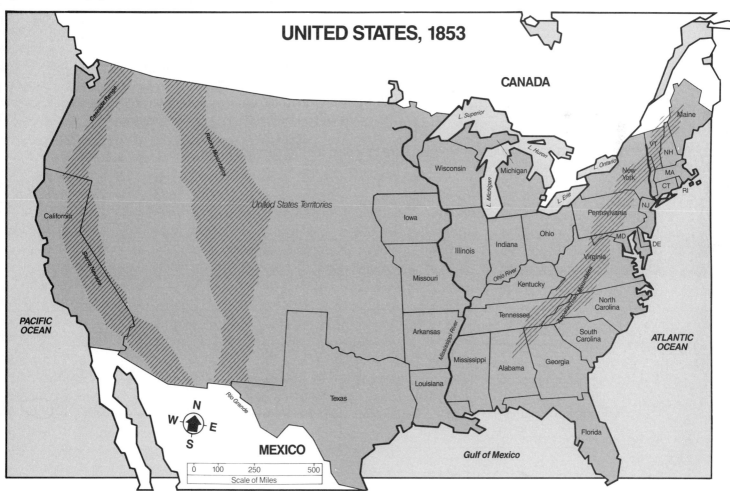

UNITED STATES, 1853

CANADA

Cascade Range

Rocky Mountains

L. Superior

L. Huron

Maine

VT

NH

MA

CT

RI

Wisconsin

Michigan

L. Michigan

L. Ontario

L. Erie

New York

United States Territories

California

Iowa

Pennsylvania

NJ

Sierra Nevada

Illinois

Indiana

Ohio

MD

DE

Missouri

Ohio River

Kentucky

Virginia

Appalachian Mountains

PACIFIC OCEAN

Arkansas

Mississippi River

Tennessee

North Carolina

South Carolina

ATLANTIC OCEAN

Mississippi

Alabama

Georgia

N W E S

Louisiana

Texas

Rio Grande

Florida

MEXICO

Gulf of Mexico

Scale of Miles
0 100 250 500

This is what the United States looked like in 1853, seventy years later.

Settling the Western Territories

BEFORE YOU READ: Vocabulary

canal	guide	log cabin	pioneer	road
frontier	log	path	plow	

Write each word next to its definition. Use a dictionary or the glossary at the end of this book if you need to. Check your answers with a friend.

1. _____ A person who shows people where to go.

2. _____ The edge of settled land.

3. _____ A house made of tree trunks or branches that are still round.

4. _____ A narrow way made by people or animals walking on it often.

5. _____ A large farm tool used to break up soil for planting.

6. _____ A cleared way on which cars, wagons, etc. travel.

7. _____ A waterway made by people and used by boats.

8. _____ Part of a cut-up tree that is still round.

9. _____ A person who does something before other people do; one of the first settlers in a new region.

Write a sentence using each of these words. Be sure that each sentence starts with a capital letter and ends with a period.

1. _____

2. _____

3. _____

4. _____

5. _____

6. _____

7. _____

8. _____

9. _____

Moving West

"The West"

At the end of the War for Independence, many Americans decided to move west. The land of the United States included more than the thirteen colonies. It also included two huge territories with more land in them than in all the colonies. These territories were west of the Appalachian Mountains. They were called the Northwest Territory and the Southwest Territory, but most people just called them "the West."

The People Who Moved West

The first people from the thirteen colonies to use this land were hunters and trappers. They used it even before the War for Independence. The next people to go to this land were farmers. Sometimes large groups of farmers moved west together. Often a guide showed them the way. These groups built their farms near one another and started towns.

We call the settlers pioneers. A pioneer is someone who does something before most other people do it.

Pioneer Life

The life of the pioneers was often hard. Most of the land in the new territories was covered with trees. The settlers had to cut down the trees before they could plant their crops. They also had to build their houses. Most of the houses were log cabins.

Pioneers made their own furniture, their own clothes, and even their own shoes. They grew corn and other vegetables, and they hunted wild animals for meat. Some pioneers brought horses or other large animals with them to pull their wagons and plows.

How the Pioneers Traveled

The first pioneers went west on foot, traveling on narrow paths made by Indians or trappers and hunters. Later they built roads. Some important roads in the United States today started as paths used by the pioneers to go west.

Some pioneers went part of the way by water. The Ohio River was the boundary, or border, between the Northwest Territory and the Southwest Territory, and boats could travel on it. In the 1820s, people started digging canals. A canal is like a river, but it is made by people. Boats on canals could carry goods and people where there were no roads.

The Frontier

When many people set up farms in an area, the hunters and trappers moved farther west. Some pioneer farmers sold their farms and moved farther west, too. They didn't like the growing towns. All through the 1800s people continued to move to the frontier, the edge of the settled land. They enjoyed living on the frontier and helping their country to grow.

UNDERSTANDING WHAT YOU READ: Using Maps

1. Scan the reading. What was the boundary between the Northwest and Southwest Territories?

   _____ . Now turn to the map of the United States in 1783 on page 13. Use two colors. Color the Northwest and Southwest Territories on the map. Color the map key to match.

2. Look at both maps on page 13. Name three states that were made from the Northwest Territory.

   _____   _____   _____

3. Name three states that were made from the Southwest Territory.

   _____   _____   _____

Daniel Boone

Daniel Boone was a famous explorer of the land west of the Appalachian Mountains. Daniel Boone was a hunter and a trapper. He was also a soldier. Daniel Boone was born in 1734. He moved west before the War for Independence. His adventures in the West show some of the things that happened when Americans settled on the frontier.

Daniel Boone was one of the first colonists to explore what is now the state of Kentucky. There were wild animals. There were also Indians who did not like the English colonists and did not want them to come into the land. But Daniel Boone lived there with his wife and children. Once some Indians captured him, but he escaped. Once Indians captured his young daughter. Daniel Boone followed the Indians and saved his daughter. He became famous as a man who could stay alive and protect his family on the dangerous frontier.

During the 1780s, Daniel Boone showed many people how to travel to Kentucky His route was called the Wilderness Road. It went from Virginia to Kentucky. It crossed the Appalachians through the Cumberland Gap, a low place in the mountains.

Daniel Boone was an excellent explorer and frontiersman, but he was a bad businessman. He owned large areas in Virginia and Kentucky, but he lost all of them because he could not prove that he owned them. Daniel Boone moved to Missouri about 1798, when it belonged to Spain. He died there in 1820.

Daniel Boone is a good example of a brave man who left his safe home in the thirteen colonies, crossed the Appalachian Mountains, and made a new home on the frontier. People who settled on the frontier, as Daniel Boone did, helped the new nation, the United States, to grow into the large country it is today.

UNDERSTANDING WHAT YOU READ: Comprehension Check

Read each statement. Write **T** for *True,* **F** for *False,* or **NG** if the information was *Not Given* in the story.

1. _____ Daniel Boone was born before the United States became independent.

2. _____ The Appalachians were very high and dangerous mountains.

3. _____ In the days of Daniel Boone, the western frontier was the Mississippi River.

4. _____ The Wilderness Road went from Virginia to Missouri.

5. _____ In those days, Kentucky was a Spanish colony.

6. _____ Daniel Boone had four children.

7. _____ A frontiersman was a person who knew how to live on land that did not have other settlers.

8. _____ Daniel Boone was a rich man because he sold his land for a lot of money.

9. _____ Daniel Boone is important in U.S. history because he helped to settle a new frontier.

10. _____ Daniel Boone could speak Indian languages.

The United States Acquires New Territories

In the beginning of 1803, the western border of the United States was the mighty Mississippi River. By 1853 the western border was the Pacific Ocean. How did the United States grow so much in just 50 years?

The United States acquired, or got, new territory in three different ways: by buying, or purchasing it; by fighting a war for it; and by making treaties or peaceful agreements with other countries.

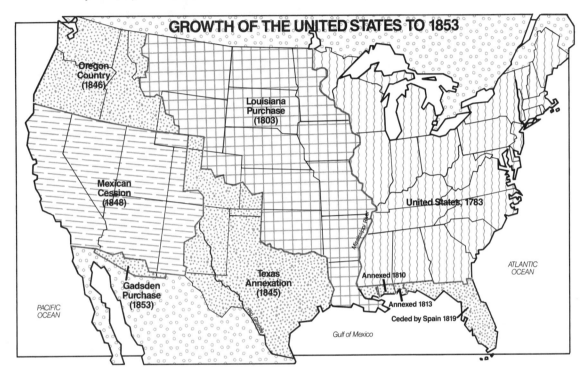

GROWTH OF THE UNITED STATES TO 1853

Oregon Country (1846)

Louisiana Purchase (1803)

Mexican Cession (1848)

United States, 1783

Texas Annexation (1845)

Annexed 1810

Gadsden Purchase (1853)

Annexed 1813

Ceded by Spain 1819

ATLANTIC OCEAN

PACIFIC OCEAN

Gulf of Mexico

MAP SKILLS

Look at the map above. It shows the territories that the United States acquired between 1803 and 1853. Use the map to answer these questions.

1. When did the United States buy the Louisiana Territory? _____

2. What do we call the land that the U.S. bought in 1853? _____

3. From what country did the U.S. acquire land in 1848? _____

    How did it acquire this land? _____

4. In what year did Texas become part of the United States? _____

5. What territory did the United States acquire in 1819? _____

6. Was the state you live in part of the U.S. in 1853? _____

    If your answer was "yes," when was your area acquired? _____

    What country claimed the land before it became part of the U.S.? _____

Land by Purchase and Treaty

The Louisiana Purchase

In 1803, President Thomas Jefferson bought for the United States an enormous area called the Louisiana Territory. He purchased this land from France for fifteen million dollars. The Louisiana Territory stretched from Canada in the north to the Gulf of Mexico in the south and as far west as the Rocky Mountains. Very little was known about it. After the Louisiana Purchase, the United States was twice as big as before.

Florida

In 1819, the United States purchased Florida from Spain. The United States had already claimed the land along the Gulf of Mexico between Florida and the mouth of the Mississippi River. The purchase of Florida made the east coast of the United States much longer.

Oregon Country

An important area that the United States acquired by treaty was the Oregon country. Both Great Britain and the United States claimed this land. In the early 1800s, only Native American Indians lived in this area, but American hunters went there to trap animals for their fur. In the 1840s, many Americans began

to travel along the Oregon Trail. (See the map on page 17.) They began to settle in the Oregon country.

Many Americans wanted Great Britain to give up its claim to the Oregon country. They wanted the United States to claim all of this land as far north as the southern tip of Alaska. But in 1846, the United States and Great Britain agreed on a treaty. It said that the United States would own the Oregon country as far north as the border between Canada and the rest of the United States. Two years later, the United States established the Oregon Territory in this area.

UNDERSTANDING WHAT YOU READ: Using Maps

Read each sentence. Decide which territory it describes: the **Louisiana Purchase, Florida,** or the **Oregon country.** Write the name of the territory on the line. The maps on pages 8–9 and on page 17 will help you find some of the answers.

1. The state of Idaho is now in this land. _____

2. This land borders the Atlantic Ocean. _____

3. This land is in the northwest corner of the United States. _____

4. The state of Kansas is now in this land. _____

5. These lands border the Gulf of Mexico. _____

6. These lands border Canada. _____

7. This land borders the Pacific Ocean. _____

8. The Rocky Mountains form the western border of this land. _____

UNDERSTANDING WHAT YOU READ: Identifying Main Ideas and Details

Read the following statements about the Oregon country. Find the statement that tells the *main idea*. Write **M** on the line in front of it. Write **D** on the lines in front of all the sentences that tell *details*.

Oregon Country

1. _____ In 1800, Indians were living in the Oregon country.

2. _____ Some Americans settled in the Oregon country before the United States acquired it.

3. _____ The U.S. acquired the Oregon country through a treaty with Great Britain.

4. _____ The north border of the Oregon country is the border between the United States and Canada.

5. _____ Some Americans were disappointed in the 1846 treaty because they wanted to claim more land.

ACTIVITY: Why Do You Think So?

Sometimes it is difficult to decide which statement is the main idea. You have to think about the whole story before you can decide on the most important point. Sometimes people have different ideas about which statement is the main idea. Sometimes both answers could be correct. The important thing is that you can give some good reasons for choosing your answer.

Sit in a small group with two or three classmates. Discuss the statements about the Oregon country. Does everyone in the group agree on the main idea? If not, tell why your answer is different from someone else's answer by filling in the lines below. If everyone agrees on the main idea, just write your reason for choosing that answer.

I said that statement _____ was the main idea about the **Oregon country,** but a classmate said

that statement _____ was the main idea. The reason for my answer is _____

_____

The reason for my classmate's answer is _____

_____

I think that _____ (I am/my classmate is) probably right.

Thomas Jefferson

BEFORE YOU READ: Using Section Headings

It is always a good idea to look over the section headings before you read a social studies text. Section headings give you clues about the information you will find in the reading. In which section of "Thomas Jefferson" would you look to find the answers to the following questions? Write the correct section heading after each question. (Do not write the answer to the question.)

1. What were the most important things Thomas Jefferson did for the United States?

    _____

2. How many years did Jefferson serve as President?

    _____

3. Was Jefferson a delegate to the Second Continental Congress?

    _____

4. What did Thomas Jefferson like to do in his free time?

    _____

5. Where did Thomas Jefferson go to school?

    _____

A Great American

Early Years

Thomas Jefferson was born in Virginia in 1743. As a young man, he went to the College of William and Mary in Williamsburg, Virginia. He graduated in 1762 when he was 19. Then he studied to become a lawyer.

Representative of the American People

In 1775, Jefferson went to the Second Continental Congress as a delegate from Virginia. The delegates at that meeting chose Jefferson to write the Declaration of Independence.

After the United States won the War for Independence, Thomas Jefferson went to France. His job was to represent the new nation in France. In 1789, George Washington was elected President of the United States. Jefferson went home to help Washington make decisions about government in the new country.

Jefferson believed that the United States Constitution needed some amendments, or improvements. He led the movement to add the Bill of Rights to the Constitution. The Bill of Rights says that the people of the United States have some very special rights and the government cannot take these rights away. In 1791, the Bill of Rights became part of the United States Constitution.

Third President of the United States

The second President of the United States was John Adams. Thomas Jefferson was elected as the third President. He was President for eight years, from 1801 to 1809.

In 1803, Jefferson bought the Louisiana Territory from France. The Louisiana Territory doubled the size of the United States. Jefferson sent the explorers Lewis and Clark to study the new territory.

Interests, Inventions, and Hobbies

After his second term as President, Jefferson returned to his home in Virginia. He continued to serve his country in many ways.

Like Benjamin Franklin, Jefferson was an inventor and a scientist. One of his inventions was a chair that revolved, or turned around. Revolving chairs are used today in offices all over the world.

Jefferson was also an architect, a person who designs buildings. He designed his own home in Virginia. His home was filled with useful inventions.

Jefferson was very interested in education. He founded the University of Virginia and designed the University buildings. Students and teachers at the University still use Jefferson's buildings.

Jefferson was interested in music. He played the violin. He spoke several languages. He was especially interested in learning more about Native American Indian languages.

Jefferson invented the money system that we use today in the United States. Jefferson's system used dollars and cents. It replaced the English system. The United States began to use Jefferson's money system in 1792.

Revolving chair

Eight-day clock

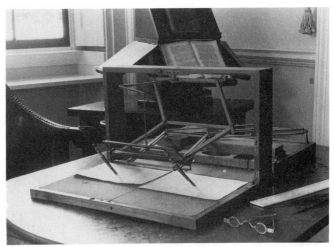
Copying machine

Jefferson and his committee present the Declaration of Independence to the Congress.

Jefferson's Gifts to His Country

Thomas Jefferson did many things for his country. He led the movement to add the Bill of Rights to the Constitution. He invented the U.S. money system of dollars and cents. As President, he bought the Louisiana Territory and doubled the size of the United States.

To many Americans, however, Jefferson's greatest contribution was made as writer of the Declaration of Independence. In the Declaration of Independence, Jefferson wrote, "We hold these truths to be self-evident, that all men are created equal, that they are endowed by their Creator with certain unalienable rights, that among these are Life, Liberty, and the pursuit of Happiness." These words set the path that the United States would follow and that it still follows today.

The Journey of Lewis and Clark

President Thomas Jefferson was very interested in the land to the west. After he bought the Louisiana Territory, he decided to send an expedition to explore this unknown area.

MAKING PREDICTIONS

Work with a partner or a small group of classmates. Write five things *you think* Jefferson wanted to know about the Louisiana Territory.

1. _____

2. _____

3. _____

4. _____

5. _____

WHAT DO YOU THINK?

For the expedition to the Louisiana Territory, Jefferson found two explorers. Their names were Meriwether Lewis and William Clark. Both men had many skills that would help them in the wilderness.

Work with your partner or group. Write four skills, or special knowledge, that *you think* an explorer needs in order to survive in the wilderness.

1. _____

2. _____

3. _____

4. _____

MAP SKILLS

Look at the map below. It shows the route, or path, Lewis and Clark followed. Write a paragraph describing the route. Be sure you mention the places and dates mentioned on the map. The first sentences are started for you.

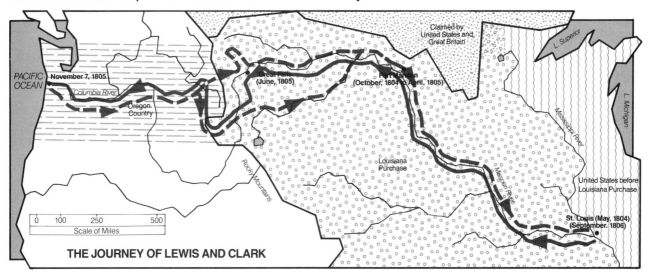

THE JOURNEY OF LEWIS AND CLARK

Lewis and Clark began their journey in May 1804. They left St. Louis and traveled up the

_____

_____

_____

_____

_____

_____

LISTENING AND TAKING NOTES

Listen to some information about the journey of Lewis and Clark. Listen carefully for the important moments in the journey. Take notes in the chart below.

THE JOURNEY OF LEWIS AND CLARK — IMPORTANT MOMENTS

What Happened	Place	Date
The first winter camp. Lewis and Clark meet Sacajawea.		
The most beautiful waterfall of the trip.		
"The most difficult part of our voyage."		
"Ocean in view! O! The joy!"		
They return to tell the news.		

Regions of the World: The Highlands

When Lewis and Clark crossed the Rocky Mountains, they were crossing a Highland Region. A highland is an area of high mountain ranges, or a long stretch of mountains that are close together.

In North America, the Rocky Mountains are the highest Highland Region. The Rocky Mountains stretch from Canada to Mexico. There are many natural resources in the Rocky Mountains. Some of these are gold, silver, lead, oil, coal, and uranium.

There are Highland Regions in many parts of the world. For example, in South America, the Andes Mountains form a Highland Region along the western coast. In Europe, the Alps are a high mountain range in Switzerland, France, and Italy. In Asia, the Himalaya Mountains form a Highland Region in Nepal and Tibet. The highest mountain in the world is in the Himalayas. It is called Mt. Everest. Mt. Everest is 29,028 feet, about 5½ miles above sea level.

In Highland Regions the climate is cool. As you go up a mountain, the temperature becomes cooler. Mount Kilimanjaro is located on the equator in Tanzania, Africa. It is about 3½ miles high. At the base, or bottom of Mount Kilimanjaro, it is hot all year round. People grow coffee at the base of the mountain. But the top of Mount Kilimanjaro is covered with ice and snow all year round.

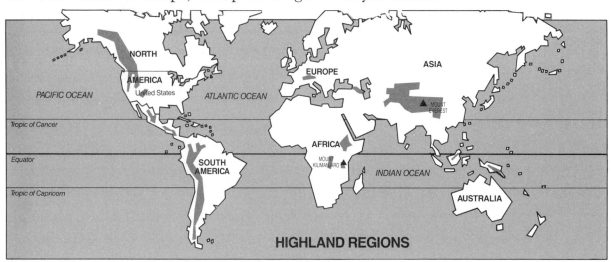

HIGHLAND REGIONS

UNDERSTANDING WHAT YOU READ: Using Maps

1. Look at the map on pages 8–9. What mountain range forms the major Highland Region in the U.S.?

   _____

2. Now look at the maps on pages 13 and 17. Explain how this Highland Region affected the westward movement of the American pioneers.

   _____

   _____

3. Do you live in a Highland Region? _____ Have you ever visited a Highland Region? _____ If your answer to either question is "yes," describe the land and the weather.

   _____

   _____

DOING RESEARCH: Using an Atlas or Almanac

Find the information that you need to complete the chart below. Some of the information is in the reading and map on page 24. Some of the information is on the maps on pages 8 and 9. However, some of the information is not in this book. You will have to look in an atlas or an almanac. Ask your teacher or school librarian to help you look up the missing information in one of these books.

Continent	A major mountain range	Highest mountain
North America		name: height: _____ feet
South America		name: height: _____ feet
Europe		name: height: _____ feet
Africa		name: height: _____ feet
Asia		name: height: _____ feet
Australia		name: height: _____ feet

Now chart the height of the tallest mountain in each continent on the bar graph below. The first example is done for you.

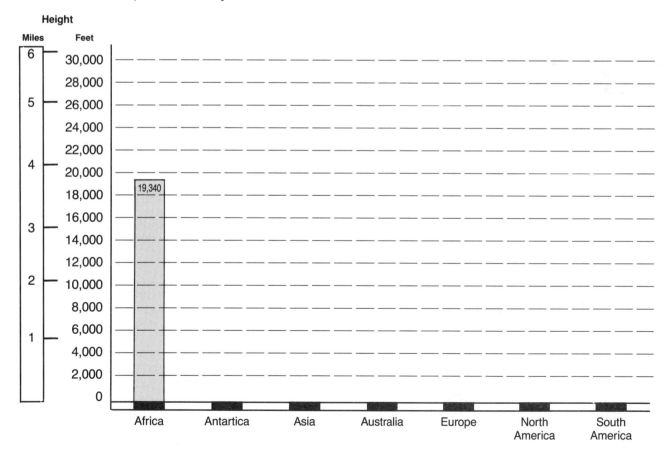

The War of 1812

After Thomas Jefferson's second term, James Madison was elected President. Like Jefferson, he served for two terms, from 1809 to 1817. While he was President, the United States went to war with Great Britain a second time. This war is called the War of 1812.

LISTENING AND TAKING NOTES

You are going to hear about the War of 1812. As you listen, take notes on the information about this war. Write your notes on the *T-list* below. The main ideas are on the left. You have to write the details on the right. Write only key words that will help you to remember the facts. You do not have to write complete sentences.

MAIN IDEA	DETAILS AND EXAMPLES
A. Three important reasons for the War of 1812.	1. British _____ stopped U.S. _____ ; made U.S. sailors _____ . 2. _____ _____ 3. _____ _____
B. An important battle inspired "The Star Spangled Banner."	1. _____ burned _____ . 2. _____ _____ _____ 3. _____ _____
C. War of 1812 changed U.S. history.	1. After war, U.S. could _____ with other _____ ; helped U.S. grow. 2. _____ _____ 3. _____ _____

The United States Develops Its Foreign Policy

doctrine	exist	foreign policy	interfere	relations

Work with a friend. Look up these vocabulary words in the glossary. Read the definitions. Then think up a sentence using each new word or phrase. Write the sentences on the lines below.

1. _____
2. _____
3. _____
4. _____
5. _____

The Monroe Doctrine

Between 1800 and 1825, most of the Spanish colonies in Central America and South America became independent. At the same time, Russia claimed part of the Oregon country in North America.

Some European countries thought that Spain should get its colonies back. People in the United States were not happy. They were friendly to the new countries in Central America and South America. And they did not want Russia to take any of the Oregon country. They wanted European countries to stay out of the Americas.

In December, 1823, President James Monroe made a speech about these things. This speech said what the relations between the United States and the European countries would be. In the speech Monroe said:

(1) European countries should not establish any new colonies in the Americas and should not try to take over countries that had once been colonies.

(2) The United States would not interfere with any European colonies that still existed and would not interfere with European governments in their own countries.

Monroe told the European countries to leave the new countries in Central America and South America alone. He said that an attack on these countries would be an attack on the safety of the United States. Monroe also told the Russians to stay out of the Oregon country.

This speech is called the Monroe Doctrine, because it was made by President Monroe. A doctrine is a statement that tells what you believe in.

Ever since 1823 the Monroe Doctrine has been part of the foreign policy of the United States. The United States still uses the Monroe Doctrine when it deals with other countries.

UNDERSTANDING WHAT YOU READ: Identifying the Main Idea

What was the main idea of the Monroe Doctrine? Circle the best answer.

a. The United States was friendly with the new countries in South and Central America.
b. The United States warned Russia to stay out of the Oregon country.
c. The United States wanted European countries to stay out of the Americas.
d. The United States promised not to interfere with European governments in their own countries.

Why People Moved West

BEFORE YOU READ: Vocabulary

Before you read "Settling the West," be sure you know these words:

ranch	a large farm for raising cattle, horses, or sheep
immigrant	a person who comes into a new country to settle and live
miner	a person who works digging minerals such as gold from the earth

Settling the West

Introduction

The road to the West was very hard and dangerous. Why did so many people leave the comfortable East and travel to the frontier in the West? There were two important reasons why many people wanted to settle in the West.

Farms and Ranches

You have already read about the first reason why people went west. It was because of the land. Thousands of pioneers, many of them immigrants from other countries, wanted to own their own land. There was rich land in the West, some of it good for farms and some of it good for ranches. People could acquire their own land by settling on it.

There were many dangers on the road to the West. Many people died on the trip. The early settlers traveled in wagons, on horses, or on foot. They traveled on roads such as the Santa Fe Trail and the Oregon Trail. Later settlers could travel by train, because there was a railroad to the Pacific coast by 1869. The trip was easier by train, and many more thousands of pioneers went west to settle in new lands.

Most Americans at that time did not think that Indians should own any land, so they thought that Indians should leave these new areas in the West. Settlers wanted to establish their farms and ranches. Often there was trouble and fighting between the settlers and Indians.

The Gold Rush

A second important reason why people went west was gold. Miners discovered gold in California in 1849, in Nevada in 1859, and in Mon-

tana in 1862. Thousands of people went west because they wanted to get rich with gold. This was the Gold Rush. About 80,000 people went to California in 1848 and 1849. They were called the "forty-niners" because they were part of the 1849 Gold Rush to California.

Some of the forty-niners went to California on the California Trail, and others got to California by boat. When many people arrived in one place, new towns started. Some of these towns are important cities today, while others became ghost towns, or towns without people, when the Gold Rush was over. Although many forty-niners found gold and became rich, most people never found any gold in the West. Instead, they built houses, settled in the new land, and started a new life.

Conclusion

There were so many people in California in 1850 that it became a state. The brave pioneers who went west and found new land or even gold were important in United States history because they settled the West and made it part of the new nation.

UNDERSTANDING WHAT YOU READ: Comprehension Check

Read the statements below. Write **T** for *True,* **F** for *False,* or **NG** if the information was *Not Given* in the story.

1. _____ The settlers found many dangers on the road to the West.

2. _____ The Santa Fe Trail was the most heavily used pioneer road.

3. _____ Many settlers went west because they wanted to have their own land.

4. _____ Indians and settlers fought over land.

5. _____ Gold was discovered in California, Nevada, and Montana.

6. _____ Many forty-niners traveled to California by train.

7. _____ Many of the forty-niners stayed and settled in the West.

8. _____ The land in California was good farmland.

9. _____ Some pioneers continued to live in ghost towns after the Gold Rush was over.

10. _____ California became the 31st state in 1850.

WHAT DO YOU THINK?

Do you think that most of the people who decided to move west were rich or poor? Why do you think so? Talk with a partner or a small group of classmates. Think of at least two reasons for your answer. Then write your answer and reasons below.

_____

_____

_____

_____

_____

_____

Regions of the World: The Mediterranean Regions

When the forty-niners arrived on the western coast of California, they found a new kind of climate. There was lots of sunshine, and it was warm all year round. The summers were dry. The winters were wetter. In fact, the climate along this part of the Pacific coast was a lot like the climate of the lands around the Mediterranean Sea. We call this type of region a Mediterranean Region.

In Mediterranean Regions, the weather is sunny and pleasant. People in these lands grow crops such as grapes, fruit trees, and olives. One problem in these lands is lack of water. Many farmers use irrigation so that their crops can have enough water. Irrigation is a way of bringing water to the fields through pipes or ditches.

Many tourists go to Mediterranean Regions. People like to spend their vacations in beautiful and sunny places. Tourists like to go to the countries around the Mediterranean Sea. They also like to go to the Mediterranean Regions of the world, such as parts of California, Chile, and Australia.

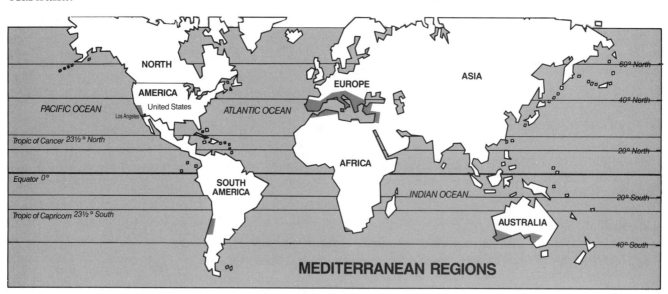

MEDITERRANEAN REGIONS

UNDERSTANDING WHAT YOU READ: Using Maps

The map on pages 10–11 will help you answer these questions.

1. Which continents surround the Mediterranean Sea? _____

2. Which continents do not have any Mediterranean Regions? _____

3. Are there any Mediterranean Regions inland? (Inland means away from a coast.) _____

MAP STUDY: Latitude Lines

Latitude lines are imaginary lines around the earth. The equator is a latitude line around the center of the earth, halfway between the North Pole and the South Pole. All the area north of the equator is called the northern hemisphere. All the area south of the equator is called the southern hemisphere.

Latitude lines are numbered in degrees. The equator is called 0° (zero degrees) latitude. Other latitude lines are drawn north and south of the equator. The North Pole is at 90° north latitude, and the South Pole is at 90° south latitude. The Tropic of Cancer is at 23½° north latitude, and the Tropic of Capricorn is at 23½° south latitude.

Use the map on page 30 to answer these questions.

1. Is the Mediterranean Sea in the northern or southern hemisphere? _____

2. Which continents have Mediterranean Regions in the southern hemisphere? _____

_____

3. Between what latitude lines (approximately) are the Mediterranean Regions in the northern hemisphere?

    Between _____ and _____ .

4. Between what latitude lines (approximately) are the Mediterranean Regions in the southern hemisphere?

    Between _____ and _____ .

ACTIVITY: Comparing and Contrasting

Los Angeles, California, is in a Mediterranean Region. You are going to compare the yearly temperature where you live with the yearly temperature in Los Angeles. You will need to look up some information in an almanac. Your teacher or school librarian will help you.

First, choose a big city near your home. (If you live near Los Angeles, choose another big city!) Look up the average yearly temperature for that nearby city in the almanac. Fill in the chart. (Remember, you have to subtract to find the temperature range.)

Los Angeles, California

Warmest month _August_	Average temperature	74°
Coolest month _January_	Average temperature	57°
Temperature range (difference between warmest and coolest)		17°

_____
(name of big city near you)

Warmest month _____	Average temperature _____	
Coolest month _____	Average temperature _____	
Temperature range (difference between warmest and coolest) _____		

Now, on a separate piece of paper, write a paragraph comparing and contrasting the weather where you live with the weather in Los Angeles. When you compare, you tell how two things are the same. When you contrast, you tell how two things are different.

Andrew Jackson

Out of the West

In 1828, the American people elected the first President to come from a western state. This President was Andrew Jackson. He came from the state of Tennessee. Andrew Jackson became the seventh President of the United States.

A Famous Soldier

Andrew Jackson was born in 1767. Before he became President, he was a lawyer, a storekeeper, and a member of Congress. He was best known as a soldier, however. He fought the British in the War for Independence when he was only 13. Later, he led American troops in the War of 1812. His troops defeated the British at the Battle of New Orleans. 2,000 British soldiers were killed or wounded. Only eight Americans were killed and thirteen were wounded. Jackson was a hero!

A Strong President

Andrew Jackson believed that the President should be a strong leader of the government. He vetoed, or stopped, more laws made by Congress than all the Presidents before him put together. He tried to get Congress to pass the laws he believed were right.

Farmers, working people, and westerners liked Jackson. They believed that he would help them. Rich people in the thirteen original states did not like him, however. They thought that Jackson would make it harder for them to make money.

Jackson and the Banks

When Jackson became President, just one bank controlled the United States money system. Jackson took away this bank's power. He made it easier for working people to borrow money from small banks. Many rich people in the Northeast were angry with this decision.

The Spoils System

Some people did not like President Jackson for another reason. When he was elected, Jackson fired many people who worked for the government. He gave their jobs to people who helped him win the election. Jackson said, "To the victor [the winner] belong the spoils [the jobs]." People call this the "spoils system." Jackson said that the spoils system was fair because it gave more people a chance to work for the government. However, many people disagreed.

The Tariff and States' Rights

Jackson made many Southern plantation owners angry because he helped pass a tariff law. A tariff is a tax on goods brought into the United States from other countries. Plantation owners wanted to buy foreign goods cheaply. The tariff raised the prices of these goods.

Some Southerners refused to obey the tariff law. President Jackson said that all states must obey the laws made by the Congress of the United States. He sent army troops to South Carolina to make sure the law was obeyed.

Native American Tribes

When Jackson was in the army, he fought against some Native American tribes. When he was President, he ordered several Indian tribes to leave their homes in the East and move to the West. Some Indian people were willing to do this, but others were not. Jackson sent U.S. army troops to the Indian homelands. The army forced the Indians to move west.

Andrew Jackson Is Remembered

Jackson was President for two terms. In 1836, he returned to his home in Tennessee. He died there in 1845.

Jackson is remembered for many things. Some people think Jackson was a very good President. Other people dislike the things he did. Most of all, Jackson is remembered because he was a strong leader. He had very strong ideas and beliefs, and while he was President he tried to get Congress and the country to follow these ideas and beliefs.

UNDERSTANDING WHAT YOU READ: Using Context

You can make a good guess about what a word means by looking at the words and sentences that come before and after the word. This is called using *context*.

Find and underline the following words in "Andrew Jackson." (On items 2, 3, and 4, look for the word in parentheses.) Then work with a partner. Decide what each word or phrase probably means. Write the definition on the line. After you are done, you can check your work by looking up the words in the glossary.

1. troops _____

2. to defeat (defeated) _____

3. to veto a law (vetoed) _____

4. to fire (fired) _____

5. foreign _____

6. to obey _____

7. to disobey _____

WHAT DO YOU THINK?

Do you think that Andrew Jackson's "spoils system" was fair or unfair? Talk with a group of classmates. Think of at least two reasons why the "spoils system" was a good idea. Think of at least two reasons why it was a bad idea. Write the reasons on the lines below.

Why the Spoils System Was Fair

_____

_____

_____

_____

Why the Spoils System Was Unfair

_____

_____

_____

_____

American Indians in the United States

1. contribution _____
2. desert _____
3. farmland _____
4. forced _____
5. homeland _____
6. journey _____
7. plains _____
8. protection _____
9. removal _____
10. trail _____

a. a very dry, sandy region with few plants

b. a trip

c. safety; something that keeps you from getting hurt

d. land where you can grow crops

e. a path or road

f. made to do something you don't want to do

g. a gift; something you give that helps someone

h. when something or someone is taken or moved away

i. a flat, grassy region

j. the place where your family and ancestors have lived for a long time

Native Americans Lose Their Homelands

The First Americans

Thousands of years before Europeans came to America, Native Americans, or American Indians lived here. There were many different tribes, or groups, of American Indians. Some Indians lived in the forests, some lived on the plains and some lived in the desert.

Europeans Change the Indian Way of Life

When Europeans came to America, American Indian life changed in many ways. Some of the changes helped the Indians, but many of the changes were not good for the Indians.

One good thing that Europeans gave to Indians was metal tools. Indians used metal tools to build homes and to cook food. Another way in which Europeans helped Indians was by giving them guns. Guns were better than bows and arrows for hunting wild animals. A very important European contribution to Indian life was the horse. With horses, Indians could travel and they could follow large herds of animals such as buffalo.

But Europeans also hurt Indians in many ways. The first colonists in the New World wanted land for themselves. They did not think that any land belonged to Indians, even though Indians were living on that land. Little by little, European settlers forced the Indians to leave their land. Sometimes they bought the land from Indians, sometimes they made agreements about land, but often they fought and killed Indians.

The Indian Removal Act

In the early 1800s, many white settlers wanted to move west of the thirteen states to the rich farmland that is now part of Alabama, Georgia, Mississippi, Tennessee, and Florida. Much of this land belonged to Indian tribes. The settlers did not want to share the land with the Indians.

In 1830, when Andrew Jackson was President, the United States Congress passed the Indian Removal Act. This law said that the Native American tribes had to leave their homes in the Southeast and move to land west of the Mississippi River. The Native Americans did not want to leave their homes, but the United States government forced them to move.

The Trail of Tears

One of the tribes, the Cherokee, went to the United States Supreme Court for protection. The Cherokee asked the Supreme Court to decide if the government was acting fairly. The Supreme Court said that the government was not being fair. White settlers did not have the right to take Cherokee lands. But the government did not listen to the Supreme Court. The President sent 7,000 soldiers to force the Cherokees to leave their homes and move west of the Mississippi. It was a terrible, difficult journey. Nearly one-fourth of the tribe died on this trip. The Cherokee called this long forced journey the "Trail of Tears."

"The Trail of Tears." In 1838, over 15,000 Cherokees were forced to leave their homes and travel west. Most of the Cherokees made the long journey on foot.

Developing Reports: Important Native Americans

RESEARCH AND WRITING

You are going to write a short report about an important Native American Indian.
Your teacher will help you choose one of the Native Americans below.

Sequoyah
(1760?–1843)

Osceola
(1803?–1838)

Black Hawk
(1767–1838)

Tecumseh
(1765?–1813)

Follow these steps to develop your report.

1. Look up information about your person and his tribe in an encyclopedia or some
   textbooks. Find the answers to these questions:
   > What tribe did he belong to?
   > Where did the tribe live?
   > Why is this person important?
   > What happened to this person's tribe in the 1800s?
   > Where does the tribe live today?

2. When you have found answers to these questions, organize your information
   into a report. Write your report on a separate piece of paper.

3. Show your report to your partner. Ask your partner to mark the places in your
   report that are hard to understand. Then talk with your partner. Explain the parts
   of the report that your partner didn't understand.

4. Next, rewrite your report. Use the lines on page 37. Think about your partner's
   comments and suggestions. Try to make the parts of the report that your partner
   marked easier to understand. Be careful with your spelling, punctuation, and
   grammar. Try to do your best work.

TITLE OF YOUR REPORT: _____

_____

_____

_____

_____

_____

_____

_____

_____

_____

_____

_____

_____

_____

_____

_____

_____

PRESENTING AN ORAL REPORT

Now you are going to present your report to a group of classmates. Practice reading your report aloud at least five times. You can practice reading it to a friend or someone in your family, or you can make a tape recording and play it back. Check these things about your oral reading:

- Do I read too fast, too slow, or about right?
- Do I read too loud, too soft, or about right?
- Do I pronounce words and phrases so that others can understand me?
- Is my report well organized so that others can follow my ideas?

When you are satisfied that you can do your best on your oral report, read it to a group of classmates who have not studied the same Native American. They will take notes on what you say.

LISTENING AND TAKING NOTES

Now listen to your classmates' reports. They will talk about three other important Native Americans. Take notes on your classmates' reports. Use the lines below and on page 39. At the end of each report, ask questions if there was something you didn't understand.

Report 1

Name of person	Date of birth/death	Name of tribe	Homeland of tribe
_____	_____	_____	_____

Why is this person important? _____

_____

_____

What happened to the tribe? _____

_____

_____

Where does the tribe live today? _____

Report 2

Name of person	Date of birth/death	Name of tribe	Homeland of tribe
_____	_____	_____	_____

Why is this person important? _____

_____

_____

What happened to the tribe? _____

_____

_____

Where does the tribe live today? _____

Report 3

Name of person	Date of birth/death	Name of tribe	Homeland of tribe
_____	_____	_____	_____

Why is this person important? _____

_____

_____

What happened to the tribe? _____

_____

Where does the tribe live today? _____

MAP SKILLS

This map shows the homelands of four Native American tribes. Use four different colors to color in the map key. Then look at your report and your notes of your classmates' reports. Find out where each tribe used to live. Then color in the homelands of the four tribes in the colors you chose for the map key.

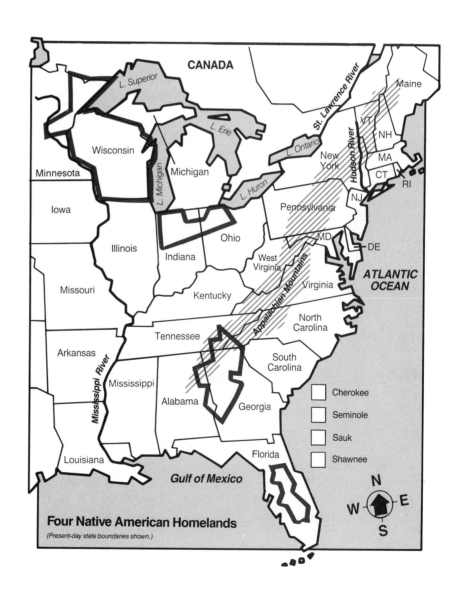

Four Native American Homelands
(Present-day state boundaries shown.)

War with Mexico

You have read about the land that the United States acquired through purchases and treaties. A third way in which the United States acquired more territory was through war. Large parts of the Southwest and West became part of the United States because of a war with Mexico.

As you remember, Mexico was a colony of Spain, but Mexico became independent from Spain in 1821. Mexican territory included what is today Texas, New Mexico, Arizona, Nevada, Utah, and California.

Although this area belonged to Mexico, many American settlers came to live there. For example, in 1823 an American named Stephen Austin led 300 families into Texas with the approval of Mexico. Ten years later there were 22,000 Americans in Texas, and they decided that they wanted to be independent from Mexico. The Texans fought against Mexico in 1836 and won. Texas was an independent country at first, but it immediately asked the United States to annex it or take it over. Congress finally agreed to annex Texas in 1845.

The United States went to war with Mexico in 1846 to decide on the border of Texas. After two years of fighting, the United States won. The border was established at the Rio Grande, the river that is still the border between the United States and Mexico. Mexico also had to sell to the

United States all of its territory in the Southwest and West. This was called the Mexican Cession. In 1853 the final border between the two countries was established when the United States bought another piece of land from Mexico. This was called the Gadsden Purchase.

The Lone Star Flag of Texas. This flag was adopted by the Republic of Texas in 1839. Today it is the state flag of Texas.

UNDERSTANDING WHAT YOU READ: Scanning for Specific Information

Find the date for each event and write it on the line in front of the statement that tells about the event.

1. _____ After fighting with Mexico, Texas became an independent republic.

2. _____ Stephen Austin brought some American settlers to Texas.

3. _____ The final border between Mexico and the United States was decided.

4. _____ 22,000 Americans were living in Texas.

5. _____ Mexico was not a Spanish colony any more.

6. _____ Mexico lost Texas.

7. _____ The war between the United States and Mexico started.

8. _____ The war between Mexico and the United States ended.

New Territories—1803–1853

Work with a classmate to make a chart that shows when the United States acquired different areas in the fifty years between 1803 and 1853. Look in these places to find the information you need:

The United States Acquires New Territories—page 17
Land by Purchase and Treaty—page 18
War with Mexico—page 40
Map of the United States Today—pages 8–9

Talk with your partner and decide which information each of you will look for. Work together as you look up the information. Use the two-letter abbreviations for the states' names. (A list of these abbreviations is at the bottom of this page.) The first one is done for you.

Date	Name of Territory	How Acquired	From Whom	Present States in Territory
1803	Louisiana Territory	purchased	France	AR, MO, IA, NE
				Most of: LA, OK,
				KS, WY, MT, SD
				Part of: CO, ND, MN
1819	_____	_____	_____	_____
1845	_____	_____	_____	_____
				_____
1846	_____	_____	_____	_____
				_____
1848	_____	_____	_____	_____
				_____
				_____
1853	_____	_____	_____	_____

Alabama	AL	Georgia	GA	Maine	ME	Nevada	NV	Oregon	OR	Virginia	VA
Alaska	AK	Hawaii	HI	Maryland	MD	New Hampshire	NH	Pennsylvania	PA	Washington	WA
Arizona	AZ	Idaho	ID	Massachusetts	MA	New Jersey	NJ	Rhode Island	RI	West Virginia	WV
Arkansas	AR	Illinois	IL	Michigan	MI	New Mexico	NM	South Carolina	SC	Wisconsin	WI
California	CA	Indiana	IN	Minnesota	MN	New York	NY	South Dakota	SD	Wyoming	WY
Colorado	CO	Iowa	IA	Mississippi	MS	North Carolina	NC	Tennessee	TN	District of	
Connecticut	CT	Kansas	KS	Missouri	MO	North Dakota	ND	Texas	TX	Columbia	DC
Delaware	DE	Kentucky	KY	Montana	MT	Ohio	OH	Utah	UT		
Florida	FL	Louisiana	LA	Nebraska	NE	Oklahoma	OK	Vermont	VT		

Eight Presidents: 1801–1850

Eight men served as President of the United States between 1801 and 1850. Listed below are some things that happened while they were President. Use the time line to answer the questions on the next page.

	President	Events
–1800		
–	Thomas Jefferson	
–		
–		1803– Louisiana Purchase.
–		1804– Lewis and Clark expedition begins.
–1805		
–		1806– Lewis and Clark expedition ends.
–		1807– Robert Fulton invents first practical steamboat.
–		
–	James Madison	
–1810		
–		1811– William Harrison defeats Shawnee Indians at Tippecanoe, IN.
–		1812– War of 1812 begins.
–		
–		1814– War ends, December 24th.
–1815		
–		
–	James Monroe	
–		
–		1819– Purchase of Florida from Spain.
–1820		1820– Missouri Compromise limits spread of slavery.
–		
–		
–		1823– Monroe Doctrine limits European colonies in the Americas.
–1825	John Quincy Adams	1825– Erie Canal opens, joining Hudson River and Lake Erie.
–		
–		
–		
–	Andrew Jackson	
–1830		
–		
–		1832– Black Hawk War. U.S. army forces Sauk Indians out of Illinois.
–		1833– First women allowed to enter college—Oberlin, Ohio.
–		1834– McCormick invents mechanical reaper to harvest grain.
–1835		1835– Florida Indians fight U.S. army to keep their land.
–		1836– Texas fights Mexico and becomes independent.
–	Martin Van Buren	
–		1838– U.S. army forces Cherokee Indians to move west.
–		
–1840	{ William Henry Harrison (Mar. 4)	
–	{ John Tyler (Apr. 4)	
–		
–		1844– Samuel Morse invents the telegraph.
–1845	James K. Polk	1845– Texas becomes the 28th state.
–		1846– Mexican War begins; Elias Howe invents the sewing machine.
–		
–		1848– Mexican War ends; gold discovered in California.
–	Zachary Taylor	
–1850		1850– California becomes the 31st state.

UNDERSTANDING TIME LINES

Use the time line on page 42 to answer these questions.

Use the time line on page 42 to answer these questions.

1. Which Presidents served two terms? _____

2. Which Presidents served less than one term? _____

3. Which President led a battle against the Shawnee Indians 29 years before he was elected?

   _____

4. When was the treaty that ended the War of 1812 signed? _____

5. Where was the Erie Canal built? _____

6. When were women first allowed to go to college? _____

7. Under what President were the Cherokee Indians forced to move west? _____

8. Who was President when Texas became a state? _____

9. Who was President when the United States went to war with Mexico? _____

10. Who was President when gold was discovered? _____

WHAT DO YOU THINK?

Four inventions are listed on the time line. Work with one or two partners. Talk about why you think each invention was important in American history. Then write your answers in the chart below.

Invention and Date	Why You Think It Was Important

A. Circle the letter of the best answer.

1. In 1783, the western boundary of the United States was the:
   a. Appalachian Mountains   **b.** Pacific Ocean   **c.** Mississippi River
   d. Rocky Mountains

2. In 1803, the United States doubled its size by purchasing:
   a. the Louisiana Territory   **b.** the Gadsden Territory   **c.** the Oregon country
   d. Texas

3. Which of the following statements about Thomas Jefferson is *not* true?
   a. He was the second President of the United States.
   b. He wrote the Declaration of Independence.   **c.** He bought the Louisiana Territory.
   d. He invented the United States money system of dollars and cents.

4. Which of the following statements about the Lewis and Clark expedition is *not* true?
   a. Lewis and Clark explored the Missouri River.
   b. Sacajawea led Lewis and Clark across the Rocky Mountains.
   c. Lewis and Clark reached the Pacific Ocean.
   d. Lewis and Clark discovered gold in California.

5. What is the best example of a highland region?
   a. the Rocky Mountains   **b.** Missouri River   **c.** Great Falls   **d.** Fort Mandan

6. Which of the following is *not* a reason for beginning the War of 1812?
   a. Great Britain stopped United States ships from going to France.
   b. Great Britain captured American sailors and made them work on British ships.
   c. The British burned the White House in Washington, D.C.
   d. Americans wanted British land in Canada.

7. The Monroe Doctrine said that:
   a. Europeans should come to the United States
   b. Europeans should adopt a new government system
   c. European governments should keep out of the Americas
   d. European governments should get back their colonies in the Americas

8. Who were the "forty-niners"?
   a. Texans who fought for independence from Mexico.
   b. Pioneers who looked for gold in California.
   c. Settlers who went with Daniel Boone into Kentucky.
   d. Explorers who went with Lewis and Clark on their expedition.

9. In the United States, the Mediterranean region is:
   a. in the Northeast   **b.** in the Southeast   **c.** in the center of the country
   d. on the West Coast

10. President Andrew Jackson used the "spoils system" to:
    a. pay the soldiers who won the battle of New Orleans
    b. give jobs to people who helped him get elected
    c. lend money to farmers and working people
    d. force Indian tribes to leave their homelands and move west

11. Which of the following is *not* related to the Cherokees?
    a. the Trail of Tears   **b.** Sequoyah   **c.** buffalo hunts   **d.** homelands in the Southeast

12. In 1846, the United States fought a war with Mexico and acquired some land. Most of this land is in what part of the country?
    a. the Southwest   **b.** the Northeast   **c.** the Southeast   **d.** the Northwest

B. Find these places on the map. Write the number of the place after each name.

Appalachian Mountains ____

Mississippi River ____

Rio Grande ____

Rocky Mountains ____

Missouri River ____

Gulf of Mexico ____

Sierra Nevada ____

Ohio River ____

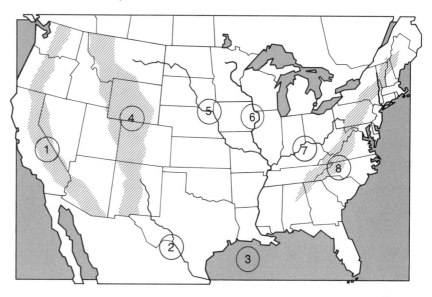

C. What Do You Think?

Discuss these questions with a friend, a small group, or the class. These are "thought questions." They do not have simple right or wrong answers.

1. Why do you think Thomas Jefferson sent Lewis and Clark to explore not only the new Louisiana Territory, but also the Spanish-owned territory west of the Rockies? Do you think Jefferson did the right thing? Why or why not?

2. "The Star Spangled Banner" was written in 1814. It became the National Anthem 117 years later, in 1931. Listen to the song and read its words. Why do you think that Congress voted to make it the National Anthem? Listen to some other songs about the United States, for example "America" ("My country, 'tis of thee . . ."), "America the Beautiful" ("Oh, beautiful for spacious skies . . ."), and "God Bless America." Do you think any of these would be a better National Anthem? Give reasons for your answer.

D. Role-Play

Work with a small group. Make up conversations that might have taken place in the following situations. Be sure everyone in your group has something to say. If you want to, write down the words you will say. After your group has practiced the conversations, perform one of your short plays for the class.

1. It is 1849. You are a small family living on the East Coast. Some of you want to leave your home and move west. Some of you want to stay. Try to make a family decision. Give reasons why you want to move west or stay in the East.

2. The time is in the 1830s. You are members of an Indian tribe. The United States government has ordered your tribe to leave your homelands and move west. Some members of your tribe have signed treaties with the government and agreed to move to the "Indian Territory" west of the Mississippi. Other members of the tribe have refused to sign and say they will fight to keep their land. Talk about what each of you will do: sign the treaty and leave your homes or stay and fight. Explain why you believe your decision is right. Try to explain to the tribe members who don't agree with you why you believe they are wrong.

The Civil War and Reconstruction

In this unit you will:

- read about the differences between the northern and southern states
- learn about Abraham Lincoln and other important Americans at this time
- find out about the major battles of the war

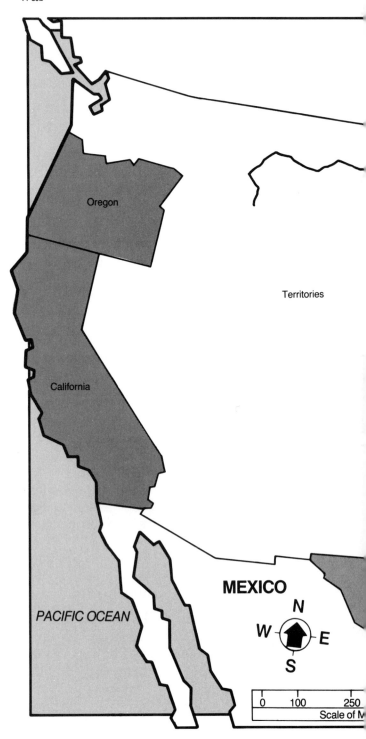

What were the causes of the American Civil War?

Where were the battles fought?

What happened to the country after the war was over?

- discuss the struggle for equal rights for all Americans: black and white, men and women
- use maps, charts, and pie graphs
- sharpen your listening, speaking, and note-taking skills
- do research and write a report

The map on these pages shows the United States during the American Civil War, 1861–1865. You will use this map as you read about the Civil War and the events leading up to it.

THE CIVIL WAR

CANADA

Minnesota

Missouri R.

Wisconsin

Michigan

Maine

VT

Hudson R.

NH

MA   Boston

New York

CT

RI

Iowa

Chicago

Pennsylvania

New York

Philadelphia

Gettysburg

NJ

DE

MD

Potomac R.

Illinois

Indiana

Ohio

West Virginia (1863)

Bull Run

Washington

Chancellorsville

Kansas

Ohio R.   Louisville

St. Louis

Kentucky

Virginia

Richmond

Petersburg

Appomatox Court House

Raleigh

Missouri

Tennessee

North Carolina

Memphis

Mississippi R.

Chattanooga

Columbia

South Carolina

Arkansas

Atlanta

Charleston

Mississippi

Alabama

Georgia

Louisiana

Vicksburg

Savannah

Texas

New Orleans

Gulf of Mexico

Florida

ATLANTIC OCEAN

500

- ◼ Union States
- ◻ Confederate States
- —— Grant's advance against Vicksburg
- - - - Sherman's march to the sea

Growing Apart

agriculture	apart	goods	income	manufacturing

Work with a friend. Look up these vocabulary words in the glossary. Then think of
a sentence using each new word or phrase. Write the sentences on the lines below.

1. _____
2. _____
3. _____
4. _____
5. _____

The South and the North

The Country Grows

People started moving to the West after the War for Independence, and this movement continued through the 1800s. California became a state in 1850. Nine years later, part of the Oregon Territory became the state of Oregon. In 1860 Kansas became the 34th state.

The United States was growing. But it was also growing apart. There had always been differences between the people in the southern states and those in the northern states. Now these differences became more important. People in the North and the South had different ways of making a living. They had different ideas about taxes. And they had a different number of representatives in Congress.

Different Ways of Making a Living

The land in the South was suited to large plantations which grew crops to sell. Most of the plantation owners grew only three major crops: cotton, tobacco, and rice. In the North, on the other hand, the land was more suited to small farms, and most farmers grew the kinds of crops they needed for their own families.

The northern states had more factories than the southern states. People in the northern states got most of their income from manufacturing, that is, from making goods in factories. People in the southern states, on the other hand, got most of their income from agriculture, that is, from raising crops.

Different Ideas About Taxes

Factory owners in the North wanted the government to tax goods that came into the United States from other countries. Goods from other countries were cheaper than goods made in the United States, but a tax on these goods would make them more expensive. If goods from other countries were more expensive, Americans would buy more goods from the factories in the North. People in the South did not want this tax. They wanted to buy cheaper goods from other countries.

Different Representation in Congress

Another difference between the North and the South was that there were more people in the northern states. The Constitution says that a state's members in the House of Representatives depend on the population of the state. The northern states had more people, so they had more representatives in Congress. When northern and southern states had different ideas about a law, the northern states usually won because they had more representatives who could vote in Congress.

These and other differences forced the northern and southern states farther and farther apart. In 1861, these differences helped to start the bloodiest war in the history of the United States.

UNDERSTANDING WHAT YOU READ: Comparing and Contrasting

List at least four differences between the northern states and the southern states.

_____

_____

_____

_____

_____

UNDERSTANDING PIE GRAPHS

A pie graph is a good way to show how big one part is compared to the whole. These pie graphs show how the House of Representatives was divided into representatives from northern states and representatives from southern states.

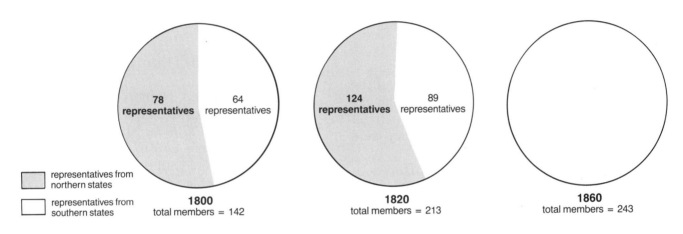

representatives from northern states		
representatives from southern states	**1800** total members = 142	**1820** total members = 213

1800 total members = 142 — 78 **representatives** / 64 representatives

1820 total members = 213 — 124 **representatives** / 89 representatives

1860 total members = 243

1. The pie graphs for 1800 and 1820 are completed. Use the information below to complete the pie graph for 1860.

    In 1860 there were 243 members in the House of Representatives. 158 of these (almost 2/3) came from "free states." 85 of these (about 1/3) came from "slave states."

2. Study the three pie graphs, then use the words in the box to complete the paragraph below. You can use some of the words more than once.

northern states	southern states	half	one-third	two-thirds

In 1800, more than _____ of the House of Representatives was made up of representatives from the _____ or "free states." Less than _____ were representatives from the _____ or "slave states." By 1820, an even greater part of the House of Representatives was controlled by the _____ . By 1860, almost _____ of the representatives came from _____ , and only about _____ came from _____ .

The Civil War and Reconstruction   **49**

Before you read the story about slavery, meet with a group of classmates. Talk about the things you already know about slavery in the United States. List some of your ideas and facts below.

1. _____
2. _____
3. _____
4. _____
5. _____

Slaves and Slavery

What Is Slavery?

There used to be slavery in many parts of the world, including the United States. Slavery means that one person owns another person. People could buy and sell slaves as if they were things and not human beings.

Slavery was one of the main differences between the southern states and the northern states. Slavery was common in the southern states, but it was rare in the northern states.

People who owned slaves did not pay their slaves any money, but they did give them a place to live, clothes to wear, and food to eat. The slaves had to work for their master, or owner, all their lives, unless their master sold them to someone else. The children of slaves were also slaves. Slave children had to work hard. Usually they did not go to school. In some states it was against the law to teach a slave to read.

Why Was Slavery Used in the Americas?

Slavery started in North and South America because the colonists from Europe needed workers for their farms and plantations. Spanish colonists made Indians work for them. Later they began to bring African slaves to work in their colonies.

The first slaves came to what is now the United States in 1619. Twenty black people were brought from Africa to Jamestown, Virginia. These people were supposed to work for the colonists for several years. Then they would be given their freedom. Most of them never became free, however.

As the years passed, farmers owned more and more land. They needed more slaves to work on the land. Between 1700 and 1800, about half a million slaves were captured in Africa and brought to the United States. Most of them were sold to farmers in the South.

The Abolitionists

Many people in the United States did not think that slavery was a good system. In fact many people, especially in the North, were against it. People who were against slavery were called "abolitionists" because they wanted to abolish, or put an end to, slavery.

Slavery was abolished, or ended, in most northern states between 1780 and 1790. Slavery was not allowed in the Northwest Territory.

From about 1820 to 1861 the disagreement about slavery became worse and worse. Most white people in the South wanted slavery to continue. They thought that slavery was necessary to help them raise their crops and make money.

Many people in the North thought that there should be no slavery in the United States. Other people in the North thought that there should be slavery only in the South.

These differences, along with the other big differences between the northern and southern states, led to war between the North and the South.

UNDERSTANDING WHAT YOU READ: Using Context

Find and underline the following vocabulary words in the story. Look at the words
and sentences that come before and after the word. Decide what the word probably
means. Write your definitions on the lines below. If you wish, work with a friend.

1. rare _____

2. harvest _____

3. captured _____

4. abolish _____

5. conflict _____

Field slaves returning from the cotton fields, 1860.

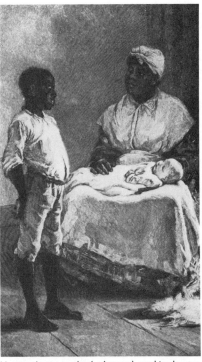

House slaves cooked, cleaned, and took care
of their master's children.

UNDERSTANDING WHAT YOU READ: Focusing on New Facts You Have Learned

What new facts have you learned about slavery in the United States? Read your
list of facts you knew *before* you read the story. Now meet with the same group
of classmates. List five new facts you have learned.

1. _____

2. _____

3. _____

4. _____

5. _____

Free States and Slave States

Slavery in 1790

In 1790, the United States had a population of nearly four million people. More than one-fifth of these people were slaves. Most of the slaves were in four states: Virginia, Maryland, North Carolina, and South Carolina. The states of Georgia and Delaware also allowed people to own slaves and to buy and sell them.

Seven states had laws against slavery. These states were New Hampshire, Massachusetts, Connecticut, Rhode Island, New York, New Jersey, and Pennsylvania.

New States

The Constitution said that new states could be admitted by Congress into the United States. Between 1790 and 1819, nine new states were admitted. Four of these, Vermont, Ohio, Indiana, and Illinois, were "free states." That is, slavery was not allowed in them. The other five, Kentucky, Tennessee, Louisiana, Mississippi, and Alabama were "slave states." These were states where slavery was allowed. This meant that there were 22 states. Half of these states were free states, and half of them were slave states.

The Problem of Missouri

When Missouri asked to be admitted as a state in 1818, many people in the North were against it. Missouri wanted to join the United States as a slave state. There would be more slave states then free states.

People made angry speeches in the Senate and the House of Representatives. Northerners said that they would vote to admit Missouri only if it came in as a free state. Southerners said that they would not let this happen.

The Missouri Compromise

In 1819, a member of the House of Representatives named Henry Clay proposed a compromise, or agreement. He said that Congress should admit Missouri as a slave state, and that at the same time it should admit Maine as a free state. Maine was part of Massachusetts, but it wanted to be a separate state. Half the states would again be free states, and half of them would be slave states.

This agreement was called the Missouri Compromise. It had one other important part. It said that slavery would not be allowed in any other new states that were north of the southern boundary of Missouri. In 1820, both the northern and southern members of Congress voted for Henry Clay's Missouri compromise, and it solved the free-state/slave-state problem for a few years.

UNDERSTANDING WHAT YOU READ: Using Maps

Choose two colors for the map key. Use the information in the story to color in the map.

FREE STATES AND SLAVE STATES AFTER THE MISSOURI COMPROMISE, 1820

☐ Free States and Territories
☐ Slave States and Territories

Harriet Tubman

Harriet Tubman was a brave black woman. She was a slave who escaped to the North. Then she helped other slaves escape to the North. She told her story to others and convinced many people that slavery was wrong.

People against slavery wanted to free the slaves. They organized the Underground Railroad. This was not a real railroad, but a chain of places to hide for slaves who ran away. People who worked in the Underground Railroad hid slaves in their homes during the day. At night, brave people like Harriet Tubman led the slaves from one safe place to another until they were in free territory.

Harriet Tubman made 19 trips to the South to help other slaves escape. This was very dangerous work, because slave owners in the South wanted to capture her. They offered $40,000 for Harriet Tubman—dead or alive. But they did not catch her, and she helped more than 300 slaves to escape to freedom.

In 1858 Harriet Tubman became a lecturer, or person who gives talks to large groups of people. Other abolitionists were also lecturers. They told people about slavery, and they tried to convince people that slavery was wrong. Because of people like Harriet Tubman, many people decided that there should be no more slavery in the United States.

Harriet Tubman (far left) and some of the slaves she led to freedom.

UNDERSTANDING WHAT YOU READ: Writing a Summary

The story about Harriet Tubman needs a concluding paragraph. A concluding paragraph tells the main ideas of a story in a few sentences. In your concluding paragraph, tell why Harriet Tubman was brave and why she was important. Start your paragraph with one of these phrases: *In conclusion, In summary,* or *The most important things to remember about Harriet Tubman are. . . .*

John Brown: Hero or Criminal?

BEFORE YOU READ: Reading for Specific Purposes

Read this story through once to understand the main ideas. You will probably read some words that you don't understand. When you have finished the story, go back and underline those words. Discuss the words with your classmates and your teacher. Try to use context and guess what the words mean. After the discussion, read the story again to understand all the details.

John Brown

John Brown was an abolitionist who was willing to do almost anything to stop slavery. He thought that slaves should revolt against their owners, just as the thirteen colonies had revolted against Britain in 1776.

John Brown began to organize a secret group of people who were against slavery. He called this secret group his "army." The people who joined him were free blacks, escaped slaves, and whites, including two of his sons.

John Brown believed that violence and force had to be used against slavery. In 1856 he killed five people in Kansas who were in favor of slavery. In 1859 his army of 18 people attacked the U.S. armory at Harper's Ferry, Virginia. The armory was where the government kept guns and other weapons. John Brown's men captured the armory and killed several people during the fighting.

John Brown believed that this violent action would make all the slaves revolt against their owners and join his army. But this did not happen. Instead, the U.S. army attacked the next day and took the armory from John Brown. Ten of John Brown's men, including his two sons, were killed. John Brown was captured. At his trial the jury decided that he was guilty of murder and treason, and so he was hanged.

After his death, many people said that John Brown was a crazy person and that he was wrong to use violence. Other people said that he was a hero and that he was right to fight against slavery.

What do you think?

John Brown's last moments before his death.

UNDERSTANDING WHAT YOU READ: Discussing and Supporting Opinions

Now you are going to discuss your ideas about John Brown with some classmates. Work in groups of three. Your teacher will tell each person what to do. One person will argue *in favor* of what John Brown did. A second person will argue *against* what John Brown did. The third person will be the mediator. A mediator makes sure that each person understands what the other person is saying. Here are the rules for your discussion.

1. Listen carefully to your classmate.
2. When your classmate has finished talking, you must summarize his or her main ideas. That is, you must say in a few words, what your classmate just said.
3. The mediator will decide if your summary is complete and correct. If it is not, you must try again.
4. If the mediator says your summary is OK, then it is your turn to say your ideas about John Brown.
5. Your classmate must listen to you carefully and then summarize your main ideas.
6. The mediator will decide if your classmate's summary is complete and correct.

WRITING A REPORT

After the discussion, you will write a short report on a separate piece of paper. The report will have four short paragraphs. In the first paragraph, briefly tell who John Brown was, what he did, and why. In the second paragraph, write why some people think John Brown was a hero. Write some of the things you and your classmates said in favor of John Brown. In the third paragraph, write why some people think John Brown was a criminal. Write some of the things you and your classmates said against him. The last paragraph is a concluding paragraph. Summarize the main ideas in the report.

Then sit in the same group of three again. Share the paragraphs you have written with your classmates. Help each other revise and edit the paragraphs. When you are satisfied with the report, copy it on the lines below.

John Brown: Hero or Criminal?

_____

_____

_____

_____

_____

_____

_____

_____

_____

_____

_____

_____

_____

_____

_____

_____

The Nation Falls Apart

The Election of 1860

In 1860, there were 18 free states and 15 slave states. Many white people in the slave states believed that they should leave the United States and start a separate country with its own laws and government.

Many other white southerners believed that the slave states should continue to be part of the United States. They hoped that people in the free states would let them keep their slaves and take them into any state in the country.

Most people in the free states believed that there should be no new slave states. Some of them thought that slavery should be ended everywhere. Many of them thought that slave owners should be allowed to keep their slaves as long as they stayed in the slave states.

These differences were important in the election of 1860.

Lincoln Wins the Election

There were four candidates, or people who hoped to be elected President, in the election of 1860. Each had different ideas about slavery. The four candidates were Stephen A. Douglas, John Breckenridge, John Bell, and Abraham Lincoln.

On November 6, 1860, Abraham Lincoln was elected as the sixteenth President of the United States. He won more votes than any other candidate. Most of Lincoln's votes came from the 18 free states.

The Southern States Secede

Abraham Lincoln believed that there should be no new slave states. He felt that the United States must stay together as one nation.

Many white southerners were afraid that Lincoln would try to interfere with slavery in the southern states. As soon as Lincoln was elected, the southern states began to secede from, or leave, the United States so they could start their own country.

By March 1861, when Lincoln's first term as President began, seven states had left the United States. Four more states seceded in the next two months. These eleven states called their new country the Confederate States of America. We often call it the Confederacy. The map shows the states that seceded and those that stayed in the Union, that is, in the United States.

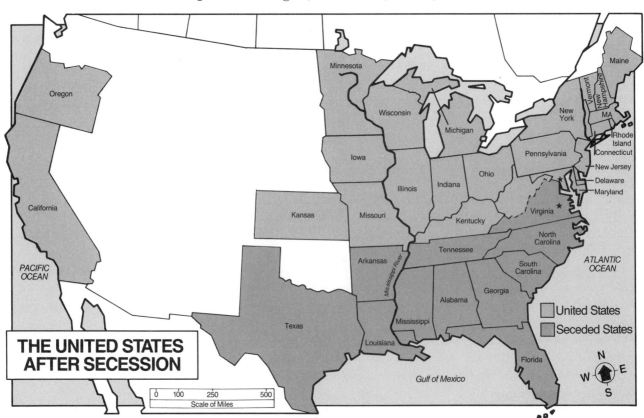

THE UNITED STATES AFTER SECESSION

USING MAPS

1. Look at the map on page 56. Find the Confederate states in the South ("Seceded states"). Write the names of two Confederate states that were on the *northern* border of the Confederacy.

   _____

2. Find the Union States in the North ("United States"). Write the names of the two Union states that were on the *southern* border of the Union states.

   _____

3. Write the names of the capitals of the Union and of the Confederacy. They are marked with stars.

   _____

4. Find the following states and color them on the map on page 56: Missouri, Kentucky, Maryland, Delaware, Virginia, North Carolina, Tennessee, Arkansas. These states are often called the "border states." Why do you think they have this name?

   _____

5. Which of the border states joined the Confederacy? Which stayed in the Union?

   Joined the Confederacy: _____

   Stayed in the Union: _____

6. Look at Virginia on the map. Notice the dotted line. The part north and west of this dotted line did not secede from the United States. The people in this part of Virginia would not join the Confederacy. In 1863, this part of Virginia became a new state called West Virginia. On the map, write WV on this part of Virginia.

7. Why do you think there were no states between Kansas and California and between Minnesota and Oregon?

   _____

   _____

   _____

8. Use the scale of miles on the map to answer these questions.

   a. About how far was it from the capital of the United States to the capital of the Confederacy?

   _____

   b. About how far was it from the capital of the Confederacy to the point farthest west in Texas?

   _____

American Civil War

Fort Sumter

Fort Sumter was a United States fort on an island in the harbor of Charleston, South Carolina. When South Carolina seceded from the Union, United States soldiers were in the fort.

When Abraham Lincoln became President, he told South Carolina that he was sending a ship to Fort Sumter with supplies. South Carolina ordered the soldiers in Fort Sumter to surrender. The commander of the fort said he would not do this. So on April 12, soldiers of South Carolina fired cannons at the fort.

Lincoln said that South Carolina had attacked the United States. He asked for 75,000 soldiers to fight against South Carolina and the other states that seceded. The Civil War had begun.

Civil War

A civil war is a war between two groups of people in the same country. The war that broke out on April 14, 1861, is usually called The Civil War, or The American Civil War, because it is the only war of this kind in the history of the United States.

The Civil War was a war between the United States of America and the Confederate States of America. As you have learned, the Confederate States of America was the name of the government set up by the seceding states. Lincoln said that the 11 Confederate states were still states of the Union, that is, of the United States. He said that they had broken the law by seceding. The Confederate leaders said that any state could leave the Union whenever it wanted to. They said that the seceding states had not broken any laws.

The Civil War lasted from 1861 to 1865. Abraham Lincoln was President of the United States all through the war. Jefferson Davis, of Mississippi, was President of the Confederacy, or the Confederate States of America.

Where the War Was Fought

The Civil War was fought almost entirely in the Confederate states. There was one battle in Pennsylvania and some fighting in Kentucky, Missouri, Ohio, and West Virginia, but most of the war took place in Virginia and along the Mississippi River in Tennessee, Arkansas, Mississippi, and Louisiana. The first big battle of the war was in Virginia. Four years later, Confederate General Lee surrendered to United States General Grant in Virginia to end the war.

The Men Who Fought the War

There were about 1½ million Union soldiers in the Civil War, and about 900,000 Confederate soldiers. At the beginning of the war, all the soldiers were white. Later, the North used black soldiers and sailors.

Both sides had good soldiers. The United States had many generals, but the one who won the most battles was Ulysses S. Grant. In 1864, he became commander of the whole Union army. The Confederacy also had many generals, but the best known one was Robert E. Lee.

More Americans were killed in the Civil War than in any other war that the United States has ever fought. The North lost about 365,000 men. The South lost about 165,000. Many of these men were killed in battle, but many more were killed by diseases.

USING MAPS

1. Look at the map on page 47. Find the capital of the Confederacy. Write the names of three battles that were fought near this city. (Battles are shown by *.)

   _____   _____   _____

2. The chart gives information about four important battles that took place in Virginia. Use the chart to answer the questions below it. Use one-word answers.

Battle	Dates	Killed and Wounded South	North	Result of Battle
Bull Run (first)	July, 1861	2,000	1,500	South won. Northern attack defeated.
Bull Run (second)	Aug., 1862	9,000	10,000	South won. Northern attack defeated.
Chancellorsville	May, 1863	10,000	11,000	South won. Northern attack defeated.
Petersburg	June 1864 to April 1865	13,000	17,000	North won. Northern attack successful.

   a. Where did the North and South have more than one battle? _____

   b. How many men from the Confederate army were killed or wounded in these four battles?

   _____ From the Union army? _____

   c. How many of these battles did the South win? _____ The North? _____

3. At the beginning of the Civil War, the Confederacy controlled the Mississippi River south of Missouri and Kentucky. General Grant led Union soldiers down the Mississippi to Vicksburg, where he won an important battle. After this, the North controlled the Mississippi. The Confederacy was split into two parts. Use the map on page 47 to answer these questions.

   a. The map shows Grant's advance against Vicksburg. Where did Grant start? _____

   b. Which three southern states were cut off from the rest of the Confederacy?

   _____   _____   _____

   c. In which direction did Grant march along the Mississippi River? _____ _____

4. United States General William Sherman won a battle against the South in Chattanooga, Tennessee, in 1863. Then he and his army marched south and east to the Atlantic Ocean. They destroyed all the houses, farms, and other buildings on this "march to the sea." Use the map on page 47 to answer these questions.

   a. At what city did Sherman first reach the Atlantic Ocean? _____

   b. Write the names of three cities that Sherman went to after he got to the sea.

   _____   _____   _____

   c. What important city in Georgia did Sherman destroy on his way to the sea? _____

5. General Robert E. Lee surrendered to General Ulysses S. Grant on April 9, 1865, at Appomattox Court House, Virginia. About how far is Appomattox Court House from the capital of the Confederacy? (Use the scale of miles on the map.) _____

Abraham Lincoln

LISTENING AND TAKING NOTES

You are going to hear about the life of Abraham Lincoln, the sixteenth President of the United States. As you listen, take notes on the information you hear. Write your notes on the T-list below.

MAIN IDEAS	DETAILS AND EXAMPLES
A. Lincoln's childhood	1. Born _____ in _____ . (date) 2. Not much _____ ; family was _____ . 3. Became a _____ .
B. Before he became President	1. Interested in _____ . 2. Elected to U.S. _____ . 3. People called him _____ . 4. Gave speeches to keep country _____ . 5. Gave speeches against _____ .
C. Election as President	1. People in North _____ . 2. White people in South _____ . 3. _____ 4. _____

D. Civil War and Emancipation Proclamation	1. Had to fight war in order to _____
	    _____ .
	 2. _____
	 3. _____
	    _____

E. End of war; end of Lincoln's life	1. Lincoln reelected in _____ . 2. _____ 3. _____

Lincoln's Words

ACTIVITY: Interpreting Historical Quotations

Lincoln was a convincing speaker. He knew how to use words that convinced people of his ideas. Read the words from Lincoln's speeches and stories below. Discuss the questions with a partner or a group of classmates. Then write your answers on the lines.

Lincoln's most famous speech was the Gettysburg Address, which he gave four months after the victory of the Union Army at Gettysburg, Pennsylvania. This is the first sentence:

> Four score and seven years ago our
> fathers brought forth on this Continent
> a new nation, conceived in liberty
> and dedicated to the proposition that
> all men are created equal.

score = twenty

conceived = begun
proposition = idea
created equal = born with the same rights

1. Lincoln gave the Gettysburg Address in 1863. What year was he talking about when he said, "Four score and seven years ago"? _____ What happened that year?

   _____

   _____

2. Why do you think that Lincoln wanted Americans to think of that year?

   _____

   _____

Lincoln liked to tell stories. One story he told was about a dream. He dreamed that he was with a group of ordinary people. One of them said about the President, "He's a common-looking man." Lincoln heard this remark. He looked at the people in the group and answered, "Common-looking people are the best in the world: that is the reason the Lord makes so many of them."

3. What does "common-looking" mean? _____

4. Lincoln's words tell us something about him as a person. In your opinion, what does this story about Lincoln's dream tell us about the man?

   _____

   _____

In March 1885, just before the Civil War was over, Lincoln gave a speech. He said:

> With malice towards none, with
> charity for all, . . . let us
> bind up the nation's wounds.

malice = desire to hurt someone
charity = love and good will
bind up = bandage

5. In your own words, tell what you think Lincoln was saying to the people of the North and the South.

   _____

   _____

Developing Reports: Three Important Americans

Many brave Americans fought on both sides of the Civil War. You have just learned about Abraham Lincoln, the President of the United States during the war. Now you will learn about three other Americans who made important contributions to American history during that time.

Frederick Douglass

Harriet Beecher Stowe

Robert E. Lee

RESEARCHING AND WRITING

Your teacher will help you choose one of the famous Americans above. You will do research on that person and take notes. Then you will write a report.

1. Look up information about your person in one or two books. You can use encyclopedias, social studies textbooks, or library books. Try to find answers to the following questions:

    When was this person born? When did he or she die?
    Where did this person live?
    During the Civil War, was this person on the side of the Union or the Confederacy?
    Why is this person famous? What did he or she do that was important? When?
    How did people in the northern and the southern states fell about this person?

    You can also take notes on any other details that you think are interesting.

2. Next, you will use your notes to write a report. Write your report on a separate piece of paper. Your report will have three parts: an **introduction,** a **body,** and a **conclusion.**

    The **introduction** is a short paragraph that tells what your report is about. Tell the name of your American and whether he or she was on the side of the Union or the Confederacy. Then in one or two sentences tell what the person did that made him or her famous.

    In the **body** of the report tell more about your person. Tell when and where he or she lived. Tell more details about the important thing(s) your person did. Tell how northerners and southerners felt about the person. Add any other interesting facts about the person.

    The **conclusion** is a final paragraph that tells the main ideas of the report. In your conclusion, tell again what your report was about and explain why your person was important in American history. Begin your concluding paragraph with one of these phrases: *In summary,* or *In conclusion* or *The most important thing to remember about. . . .*

3. Share your report with a classmate who has written about the same person. Ask your partner to read your report and mark the places that are hard to understand. Discuss these parts with your partner. Together, think of ways to make those sentences clearer.

4. Next, rewrite your report. Use the lines on page 63. Think about your classmate's suggestions. Be careful with your spelling, punctuation and grammar. Try to do your best work.

TITLE OF YOUR REPORT: _____

_____

_____

_____

_____

_____

_____

_____

_____

_____

_____

_____

_____

_____

_____

_____

_____

_____

_____

_____

_____

_____

_____

_____

_____

_____

PRESENTING AN ORAL REPORT

Now you are going to present your report to a group of classmates. Practice reading your report aloud at least five times. Read it to a friend or someone in your family, or make a tape recording and play it back. Check these things:

- Do I read too fast, too slow, or about right?
- Do I read too loud, too soft, or about right?
- Do I pronounce words and phrases so that others can understand me?

When you are satisfied that you can do your best on your oral report, read it to a group of classmates who have not studied the same American. They will take notes on what you say.

LISTENING AND TAKING NOTES

Now listen to your classmates' reports. They will talk about two other important Americans. Take notes on your classmates' reports. Use the lines below. At the end of each report, ask questions if there was something you didn't understand.

Report 1

Name of person _____

Which side was this person on? _____

Why is this person important in American history? _____

_____

_____

_____

_____

What did people in the North and South think about this person? _____

_____

_____

Report 2

Name of person _____

Which side was this person on? _____

Why is this person important in American history? _____

_____

_____

_____

_____

What did people in the North and South think about this person? _____

_____

_____

UNDERSTANDING WHAT YOU READ: Interpreting Historical Quotations

Read the sentences below. Who do you think the words were spoken by, or spoken about? Choose between the three famous Americans you have just studied: **Frederick Douglass, Robert E. Lee,** and **Harriet Beecher Stowe.**

When President Lincoln met this person he said, "So this is the little lady who started the Civil War."

1. Who was Lincoln talking about? _____

2. Why did he say this person had started the war? _____

_____

_____

"I had to meet the question whether I should take part against my native state. With all my devotion to the Union, and the feeling of loyalty and duty of an American citizen, I have not been able to make up my mind to raise my hand against my relatives, my children, my home. I have therefore resigned my commission in the army, and, save in defense of my native state—I hope I may never be called upon to draw my sword."

3. Who do you think said these sentences? _____

4. How do you think this person felt about the fact that the southern states seceded? _____

_____

_____

_____

"Colored men going into the Army and Navy must expect annoyance—but let no man hold back on this account. We shall be fighting a double battle, against slavery in the South and against prejudice . . . in the North, and the case presents the very best assurances of success."

5. Who do you think wrote these words? _____

6. Did this person think that black Americans should join the Union army? _____

7. Why did this person think life in the army would be particularly hard for black soldiers?

_____

_____

Putting the Nation Back Together

The Problem

The Civil War ended in 1865, but this was not the end of problems for the United States. The nation had to be reunited, or put back together again.

Lincoln wanted to reunite the nation quickly. He wanted to pardon, or forgive, the South for leaving the Union. After Lincoln was killed, Andrew Johnson became President. He tried to carry out Lincoln's plans. He said that the seceded states could come back into the Union if they would ratify the 13th Amendment to the U.S. Constitution and obey the laws of the United States. All the states agreed.

Congress Fights the President

Many people in Congress were not happy with Johnson's plans. They said that only Congress could let the states come back into the Union. They set up their own plan. When President Johnson objected, they tried to remove him. The Constitution says that the House of Representatives can "impeach," or accuse, the President. The Senate then votes on whether to remove the President. The House impeached Johnson, but the Senate, by one vote, let him remain as President.

The Reconstruction Period

The period from 1865 to 1877 is called the Reconstruction period. Reconstruction means rebuilding or building again. The aim of Reconstruction was to rebuild the United States. The eleven states that had seceded had to be brought back into the Union.

Congress said the states must hold conventions to write new state constitutions. Nobody who had fought in the Confederate army could vote for the delegates to these conventions. Between 1868 and 1870, Congress approved the new constitutions.

Congress also sent United States soldiers into the South. These soldiers protected the new state governments. Men who had been Confederate leaders could not take part in the government of their own states. Northerners came to the South and took some government jobs. People in the South called these northerners "carpetbaggers," because they brought their clothes in big bags made out of pieces of rugs or carpets.

Three Amendments to the Constitution

During this period, Congress proposed three amendments to the Constitution. For an amendment to become part of the Constitution, it must be ratified, or approved, by three-fourths (3/4) of the states. All three amendments were quickly ratified. The seceding states were told that they had to ratify these amendments in order to be readmitted to the Union. Here is what the amendments said:

13th Amendment (1865)—Abolition of Slavery. This amendment said there would be no more slavery in the United States.

14th Amendment (1868)—Citizenship. This amendment said that everyone in the United States was a citizen and had the same rights as all other citizens.

15th Amendment (1870)—Right to Vote. This amendment said that a person's right to vote could not be taken away because of that person's race or color or because that person had been a slave.

The End of Reconstruction

Reconstruction was a very hard time for most people in the South. Most of the fighting in the Civil War had been in the South, and many cities, towns, roads, railroads, and bridges had been destroyed. Most white southerners did not like the new state governments that the Union set up. Many of them did not like the fact that black people were citizens and that black men could vote.

Slowly, however, the South regained control of its state governments. By 1877, all the Union soldiers had left the South. Southerners could again govern themselves. This ended the period of Reconstruction.

ACTIVITY: Build Your Vocabulary

In the first paragraph of "Putting the Nation Back Together," you find this sentence: "The nation had to be reunited or put back together again."

1. What does *reunited* mean? _____

2. Now look at the fourth paragraph. What does *rebuilding* mean? _____
_____

3. The last paragraph says that the South regained control of its state governments. What does *regained* mean? _____

4. When you see the prefix *re-* in front of a verb, what does it probably mean? _____
_____

5. Now write the meaning of each of these words:

   reconstruct _____

   review _____

   readmit _____

   review _____

   reelect _____

UNDERSTANDING WHAT YOU READ: Thinking About Reconstruction

Work with a partner or a small group of classmates. Write the answers to these questions.

1. Why do you think it was necessary, after the Civil War, to "rebuild the United States"? What kinds of things had to be rebuilt? Think of *intangibles*—that is, things that cannot be touched, handled, or seen—as well as *tangibles*, things that *can* be touched, handled, or seen.

   _____

   _____

   _____

2. Why do you think Lincoln wanted to pardon the South? _____

   _____

   _____

   _____

3. What do you think happened in the South after the United States soldiers left in 1877?

   _____

   _____

   _____

   _____

After Slavery: The Problems of the Free Blacks

Finding Work

The 13th Amendment was ratified in 1865. It ended slavery throughout the United States. It also brought with it a whole new set of problems for the people who had been slaves.

These free blacks no longer had to work for their masters. But their masters no longer had to give them food and clothing and a place to live. The slaves were free, but they did not own any land. They had no money to buy land or start a business. Most of them could not read or write. How did they survive?

Many free blacks stayed on the plantations where they had been slaves. However, many of the plantation owners could not pay their workers. So they used a system called sharecropping. In this system the plantation owners rented land to blacks and other poor people. These sharecroppers, as they were called, raised crops on the land. They gave a part, or share, of the crops to the plantation owners to pay the rent. This system helped both the blacks and the plantation owners to survive.

The Black Codes

In 1865, President Andrew Johnson quickly let the seceded states come back into the Union. The leaders of these states were men who had fought against the Union in the Civil War. One of the first things these men did was to pass state laws called "Black Codes." These laws told what blacks could and could not do. The codes said that blacks were free, but that they were not equal to white and were not citizens of the United States.

When Congress set up its own Reconstruction plan, the Black Codes were repealed, or abolished. When the 14th and 15th Amendments to the Constitution were ratified, blacks became citizens and could vote.

The Freedmen's Bureau

A month before the end of the war, Congress established the Freedmen's Bureau. This was an organization to help freed slaves and poor southern whites. The Freedmen's Bureau gave food and health care to these people, and helped them to find jobs.

The Freedmen's Bureau also started several black colleges and universities in the South. These colleges and universities educated many black leaders and teachers. The Freedmen's Bureau helped freed slaves to use their new rights. Blacks began to vote. For the first time, blacks were elected to government jobs in the South.

Segregation

The Reconstruction period ended in 1877. Southern whites regained control of their state governments. Soon they began to take away many of the rights that the blacks had. They made laws that segregated blacks, that is, that separated them from whites. Blacks had to sit in separate places from whites in trains, churches, and other places. Blacks had to go to separate schools from whites.

When black people tried to use the rights that the 14th and 15th Amendments gave them, southern whites used violence to stop them.

Black Rights Today

It took many years for blacks to regain, or get back, their rights. In 1954, more than 70 years after the end of Reconstruction, the United States Supreme Court said that schools could not be segregated. Students of all races had the right to go to any school. In 1957, Congress passed a Civil Rights Act and a Voting Rights Act. In 1964, it passed another Civil Rights Act. These laws helped to change the way blacks were treated in all parts of the United States.

UNDERSTANDING WHAT YOU READ: Summarizing

Now sit with a group of classmates and discuss the important facts you learned from the reading. Then, on a separate piece of paper, write a summary in your own words about the main problems of the free blacks.

UNDERSTANDING WHAT YOU READ: Unit Vocabulary Review

Use words from the box to complete the crossword puzzle.

Amendment
candidates
Confederacy
free
harvest
hero
injustice
plantation
poor
population
ratify
Reconstruction
rent
repeal
rights
secede
segregation
sharecropper
slave
slavery
survive
tariff
unequal
Union
unite
your

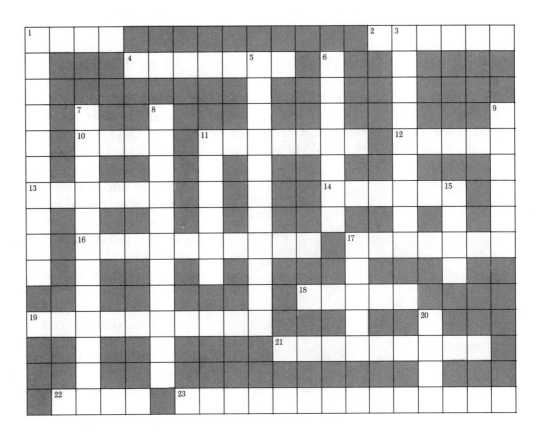

ACROSS
1. Having little or no money.
2. The 14th Amendment said that all Americans, black or white, had the same _____ .
4. To pick or gather crops.
10. A person who does brave things and is admired by other people.
11. To go through hard times and come out alive.
12. A person who is owned by another person.
13. A tax on goods made in other countries and then sold in the United States.
14. To approve a law by voting for it.
16. There were four _____ in the Presidential election of 1860.
17. Not the same (in size or treatment, for example).
18. To join together.
19. The number of people in a place such as a city, state, or country.
21. The 13th _____ ended slavery in the United States.
22. After the Civil War, the slaves were _____ .
23. The rebuilding of the South after the Civil War.

DOWN
1. A very large farm where only one crop is grown.
3. Unfairness.
5. Under _____ , black children have to go to different schools from the ones that white children go to.
6. A system in which one person can own another person.
7. A _____ rented land from a plantation owner and gave some of the crops to the owner as rent.
8. During the Civil War, the southern states were called the _____ .
9. To vote out, or do away with, a law.
11. When Lincoln was elected President, eleven southern states decided to _____ .
15. Belonging to you.
17. During the Civil War, the northern states were called the _____ .
20. To pay money in order to live in a house or use land or property owned by someone else.

Some Famous Black Americans

Three Well-Known Black Americans

Some blacks, such as Frederick Douglass and Harriet Tubman, were well known before the Civil War. After the end of slavery, more black Americans played important roles in the history of this country. Three of these famous black Americans were Sojourner Truth, Booker T. Washington, and W.E.B. Du Bois. All three helped black people understand the kinds of things they could do with their lives as free men and women.

Sojourner Truth

Sojourner Truth's real name was Isabella Baumfree. She was born a slave in New York state in about 1797. When she was 30, the state of New York abolished slavery. Her owner refused to let her be free, so she ran away.

When she was 44, Isabella changed her name to Sojourner Truth and began to make speeches against slavery. No black woman had ever done this. She spoke in cities all over the North.

Sojourner Truth was a tall woman with a deep voice. She knew how to use words to make people believe in her ideas. When she got up to speak, people listened!

Sojourner Truth believed that neither women nor slaves had the rights that they should have as human beings. She began to make speeches about women's rights as well as speeches about slavery.

During the Civil War, Sojourner Truth worked in Union hospitals. In 1864, she visited President Lincoln at the White House. After the war, she taught freed slaves and helped them to find jobs. She died in Michigan in 1883 at the age of 86.

Booker T. Washington

Booker T. Washington was also born a slave, but he became free at the age of nine, when the 13th Amendment was ratified. When he was 16, he went to Hampton Institute, a school for blacks in Virginia. Hampton Institute taught skills to help young blacks get good jobs in factories and businesses.

In 1881, Booker T. Washington started a school for black people in Tuskegee, Alabama. Tuskegee Institute, as it is now called, taught factory and business skills just as Hampton did, but it also trained teachers and farmers.

Booker T. Washington believed that blacks needed job skills so that they could get good jobs and buy their own homes, farms, and businesses. He thought that later, white Americans would give blacks equal rights. But first, he believed, blacks had to prove that they could work hard and earn money. Many white people agreed with Washington. President Theodore Roosevelt and President William Howard Taft asked Booker T. Washington to help them make decisions about the treatment of black people.

W.E.B. Du Bois

One man who did not agree with Booker T. Washington was another black named W.E.B. Du Bois. Du Bois said that blacks must demand equal rights now. He believed that black Americans would never get equal rights unless strong, well-educated, black leaders helped them to fight for those rights.

Du Bois himself was a strong, well-educated, black leader. He was born in Massachusetts in 1868, three years after the end of the Civil War. He graduated from Fisk University, a black college in Tennessee. Then he went on to study at Harvard University in Massachusetts. He became a college professor and a writer. In 1909, with other black leaders, he started the National Association for the Advancement of Colored People (NAACP) to work for equal rights for all blacks. The NAACP is still a strong organization today.

Dr. Du Bois wrote many magazine articles and books about the life of black people in America. People all over the world still read his books. Du Bois died in Ghana, Africa, in 1963, at the age of 95.

UNDERSTANDING WHAT YOU READ: Comprehension Check

Read the statements below. For some of the statements you will need to think about facts you learned on pages 66 and 70. Write **T** for *True,* **F** for *False,* or **NG** if the information is *Not Given.*

Booker T. Washington

1. _____ Before the Civil War many black women traveled to northern cities and gave speeches against slavery.

2. _____ In 1800, slavery was allowed in New York state.

3. _____ Sojourner Truth never traveled to the southern states.

4. _____ Sojourner Truth voted for Lincoln in the 1860 election.

5. _____ Booker T. Washington was born in 1856.

6. _____ Tuskegee Institute taught black students how to become better farmers, how to work with machines, and how to run a small business.

7. _____ Booker T. Washington and W.E.B. Du Bois were both born in southern states.

8. _____ W.E.B. Du Bois is still alive today.

9. _____ The NAACP is an organization that works to get equal rights for black Americans.

10. _____ Sojourner Truth joined the NAACP.

Now look back at the information on pages 66 and 70 to check your answers.

UNDERSTANDING WHAT YOU READ: Comparing and Contrasting

Work with a friend. Try to think of as many different answers as you can.

1. List some ways Booker T. Washington and W.E.B. Du Bois were alike.

_____

_____

_____

W.E.B. DuBois

2. List some ways Booker T. Washington and W.E.B. Du Bois were different.

_____

_____

_____

_____

The Civil War and Reconstruction   **71**

Women in United States History

Colonial Women

Women have always been important in American history, but they have not always had the same rights as men.

Women helped to establish the early colonies in Virginia and Massachusetts. They worked extremely hard for the colonies, but they weren't allowed to be leaders in government, religion, or business.

Pioneer Women

When people in United States began to settle in the West, pioneer women did the same work as men. They cleared the land, they helped build houses, and they fought against people who attacked their homes.

The Women's Rights Movement

In the 1800s, many men and women began to work for equal rights for women. These were often the same people who felt strongly about freedom of black Americans. For example, both Frederick Douglass and Sojourner Truth wrote and spoke out about women's rights as well as about the rights of blacks.

In 1848, a Women's Rights Convention was held in Seneca Falls, New York. The people at this convention wrote a Declaration of Sentiments which told what they believed. The Declaration began, "We hold these truths to be self-evident, that all men and women are created equal."

Two important leaders in the Women's Rights movement were Susan B. Anthony and Elizabeth Cady Stanton. In 1869, they organized the National Woman Suffrage Association. This organization worked to get suffrage, or the right to vote, for women.

The Right to Vote

At first, only white men who owned property and paid taxes could vote in most states. Later, most states allowed all white men to vote. In 1870, the 15th Amendment said that states must let black men vote. But no state said that women could vote.

In 1869, the Territory of Wyoming, which was not yet a state, said that women could vote. By 1920, more than half of the states allowed women to vote. Then, in that year, the 19th Amendment was adopted. This amendment said that a state could not keep a person from voting just because she was a woman. For the first time, all women in the United States could vote.

1920—Women win the right to register and vote.

Some Famous American Women

Some women became very well-known in the 1800s. Harriet Beecher Stowe was famous as the author of *Uncle Tom's Cabin* and other books. Helen Hunt Jackson wrote about the way Native American Indians were treated. Mary Lyon started the first college for women. Emily Dickinson became known for the many poems she wrote. Some people think that she is America's greatest poet.

Other well-known American women of the 1800s include Elizabeth Blackwell, the first woman doctor to graduate from a U.S. medical school, and Maria Mitchell, the first woman to teach astronomy in a college. American women also became known in art and music. Mary Cassatt was a famous painter, and Amy Beach (Mrs. H.H.A. Beach) was a well-known composer.

UNDERSTANDING WHAT YOU READ: Using Maps

Woman Suffrage Before 1920

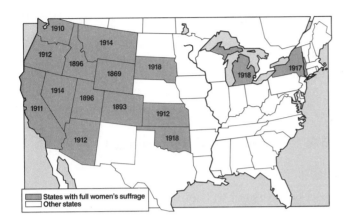

States with full women's suffrage
Other states

In 1920, the 19th Amendment gave women in all states the right to vote. However, in many states, women had the right to vote before the 19th Amendment was law.

1. When were women first allowed to vote in your state? _____

2. Which states gave women the right to vote before 1900? _____
_____

3. In what part of the country were these states? _____

4. Which part of the country was last to give women the right to vote? _____
_____

WHAT DO YOU THINK?

Work with a partner or a small group of classmates. Answer these questions.

1. The Declaration of Sentiments written at the Women's Rights Convention in 1848 begins with a sentence that is very similar to the first sentence of another important American document. What document is that? How are the first sentences of these two documents different?

_____
_____

2. Why do you think the right to vote was such an important right for women and blacks to win?

_____
_____
_____

3. Why do you think the newer western states were quicker to give women suffrage?

_____
_____

A. Circle the letter of the best answer.

1. The main reason that there was slavery in the United States was that:
   a. plantation owners needed workers for their land
   b. almost everybody had slaves in those days
   c. it was cheaper because slaves had very low salaries
   d. slaves were very good farmers

2. An abolitionist was someone who wanted to:
   a. own slaves   b. sell slaves   c. free slaves   d. abolish the government

3. The Underground Railroad:
   a. went under the Potomac River   b. helped workers get to their jobs
   c. helped slaves escape to freedom   d. carried supplies to the South

4. John Brown:
   a. owned 18 slaves   b. worked in the armory at Harper's Ferry
   c. was killed in a battle at Harper's Ferry   d. wanted slaves to revolt

5. Abraham Lincoln wanted the:
   a. South to be an independent country   b. United States to be one country
   c. North to have slavery   d. West to join the United States

6. The Civil War started in:
   a. 1776   b. 1819   c. 1861   d. 1877

7. The states in the South that fought in the Civil War were called the:
   a. United States   b. Union   c. border states   d. Confederacy

8. Most of the Civil War battles were fought:
   a. in the northern states   b. in the southern states
   c. in the western states   d. on the ocean

9. The Emancipation Proclamation said that:
   a. all citizens could vote   b. the Civil War was over
   c. slaves in the South were free   d. the South surrendered to the North

10. The period of rebuilding the South after the Civil War was called:
    a. sharecropping   b. Reconstruction   c. suffrage   d. emancipation

B. Match each Constitutional amendment with its correct description.

1. 13th Amendment _____   a. Black American men were given the right to vote.

2. 15th Amendment _____   b. All American women were given the right to vote.

3. 19th Amendment _____   c. There would be no more slavery in the United States.

C. Write one or two sentences about each of these famous Americans. Tell who he or she was and what he or she did.

1. Harriet Tubman _____

_____

2. Harriet Beecher Stowe _____

_____

3. Ulysses S. Grant _____

_____

4. Robert E. Lee _____

_____

5. Booker T. Washington _____

_____

6. Susan B. Anthony _____

_____

D. What Do You Think?

Discuss these questions with a friend, a small group, or the class.

1. Why do you think most of the fighting in the Civil War took place in the Confederate states? (Hint: What do you think the two sides were fighting for?)
2. In this unit you have learned about several famous Americans. Which one do you admire most? Why?

E. Role-Play

Work with a small group. Make up a conversation that might have taken place in the following situation. Be sure everyone in your group has something to say. If you want to, write down the words you will say. After your group has practiced the conversation, perform your short play for the class.

The years of Civil War were very difficult times for the United States. The country was divided, and brothers sometimes fought on opposite sides in the battles. Imagine you are a family living in one of the border states. Some of you believe your state should secede and join the Confederacy. Others of you feel that you must stay loyal to the Union. Talk about your opinions. Try to convince the other members of your family to agree with you.

The Age of Industry

In this unit you will:

- read about the ways in which the United States grew after the Civil War
- learn about some important industries and inventions
- learn about the Grassland and Desert Regions
- find out about Sitting Bull, an important Native American Indian

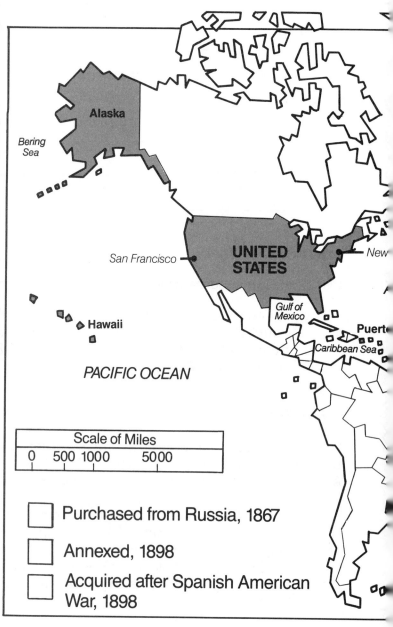

What was "The Gilded Age"?

What was the Industrial Revolution and what changes did it bring?

What happened to the Native American Indians after the Civil War?

- study some people who tried to help workers and poor people
- make a family tree
- use maps, charts, and graphs
- sharpen your listening, speaking and note-taking skills

The map on these pages shows the lands that the United States gained in the last part of the nineteenth century. You will use this map as you read about the ways in which the United States grew in the period from 1865 to 1900.

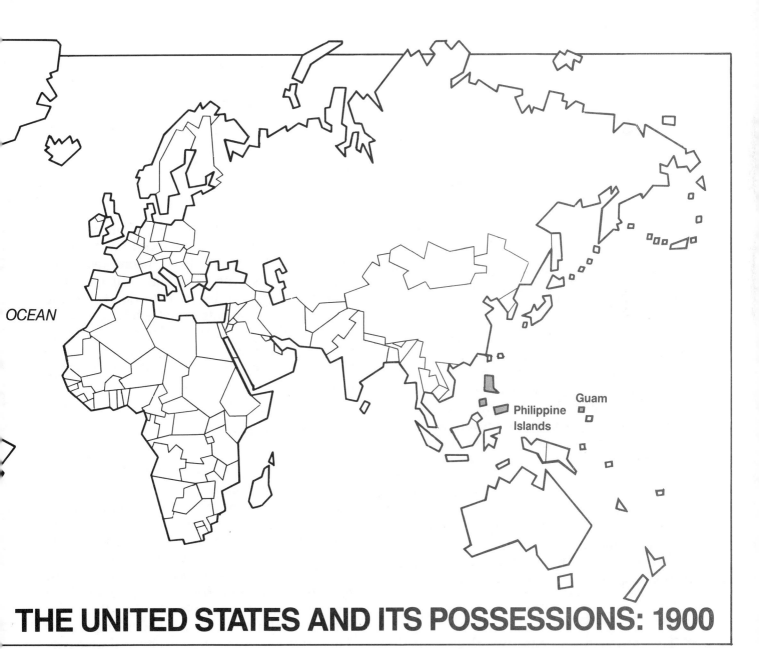

OCEAN

Philippine Islands

Guam

THE UNITED STATES AND ITS POSSESSIONS: 1900

The United States Continues to Grow and Change

Growing Again: 1865–1900

The United States Grows in Many Ways

After the Civil War, the United States picked itself up and started growing again. In 1867, the United States bought Alaska from Russia. In 1898, it annexed Hawaii. Also in 1898, the United States fought a war with Spain. As a result of the Spanish-American War, the United States acquired the Philippine Islands and the islands of Puerto Rico and Guam.

The United States grew in other ways, too. It grew in population: between 1870 and 1900 the population nearly doubled. It grew in power: its navy was the third largest in the world in 1900. And it grew in wealth: its industries made enormous fortunes for some of its people, and its manufactured products were used all over the world.

Finally, the United States grew in literature and art. United States writers, painters, and architects were admired not only by Americans but by people from other countries as well.

Weak Presidents

The growth in power and wealth and population took place without any strong Presidents to guide it. After Abraham Lincoln, most of the Presidents were quite weak. Andrew Johnson, who became President when Lincoln was killed, tried to be a strong President, but Congress stopped everything he tried to do. Following Johnson, the Presidents were General Ulysses S. Grant, Rutherford B. Hayes, James A. Garfield, Chester A. Arthur, Grover Cleveland, and Benjamin Harrison. None of these was a strong leader.

Corrupt Government

During these years there was much corruption in government, that is, many government workers were dishonest. Some of them stole money from the government. Others made decisions that would help people who gave them bribes, that is, who paid them money secretly. General Grant's eight years as President were especially corrupt. Grant himself was an honest man, but many of the friends that he gave jobs to were not honest. Even Grant's Vice-President, Schuyler Colfax, was accused of taking bribes. There was also corruption in city and state governments.

The Rich and the Poor

Enormous fortunes were made between 1865 and 1900. John D. Rockefeller made a billion dollars in the oil industry. Andrew Carnegie made hundreds of millions of dollars in the steel industry. Willam H. Vanderbilt made more millions in railroads. These were only a few of the many who got very, very rich during this period.

Most Americans did not get rich, however. Millions of men and women worked in noisy, dirty factories for 12 to 14 hours a day for very little money. Many of these workers were immigrants who came from other countries. Some people weren't able to find work and had no money at all. Many Americans lived in crowded, cold apartments without running water or heat.

The Gilded Age

A popular book published in the 1870s was called *The Gilded Age*. To gild something is to put a thin layer of gold on it so that it looks as if it is made out of gold. Underneath the gold, however, there is just ordinary wood, plaster, or tin. The period from 1865 to 1900 was like this. What many people saw was the great houses of the wealthy, their powerful steam yachts, and the huge parties that they gave for one another. But underneath all this was greed, corruption, and poverty. There was a huge gap between the rich and the poor. This was the Gilded Age.

UNDERSTANDING WHAT YOU READ: Summarizing

1. List at least four ways in which the United States grew from 1865 to 1900.

_____   _____

_____   _____

_____   _____

2. List at least three problems the United States had during this time.

_____   _____

_____   _____

3. Name three men who became very wealthy during this period. Tell how they made their money.

_____

_____

_____

4. Why was this period of United States history called "The Gilded Age"?

_____

_____

UNDERSTANDING WHAT YOU READ: Using Maps

Turn to the map on page 77. Color in the new territory the United States acquired between 1867 and 1900. Remember to color the map key, as well.

The Industrial Revolution

The Textile Industry

The first industry that used machines in the United States was the textile industry. The first textile factory opened in 1790. Fifty years later, in 1840, there were 1200 textile factories in the United States. Most of these were in the Northeast.

Towns and cities grew up around the factories. The factories made cloth from the cotton grown in the South. The textile factory workers were mostly women. These women left the farms where they grew up and moved to the cities.

The Railroads

The first railroad companies started in 1830 in South Carolina and Maryland. By 1836, there were railroads in eleven states, with more than a thousand miles of track.

In 1869, a railroad across the whole country was completed. It connected the East Coast to the West Coast. Many of the people who built this railroad were immigrants from China. Railroads to the West made it easy for people from the East to settle in the West. The railroads also carried products made by the factories and crops grown on the farms and plantations.

What Was The Industrial Revolution?

A revolution is a complete change in something. The War for Independence, which started in 1775, is called the American Revolution because it was a complete change in government. At about the same time as the American Revolution, another revolution was starting. This was the Industrial Revolution.

The Industrial Revolution was a complete change in the way that things were made. Before the Industrial Revolution, most things were made by hand in people's homes or in small shops. After the Industrial Revolution, most things were made by machines in factories. The machines could make things faster and more cheaply.

Four Important Industries

You are going to read about four important industries that developed during the Industrial Revolution and about some of the changes that these industries made in the United States. The four industries are *textiles*, or the making of cloth, *railroads*, *steel*, and *oil*.

Chinese workers help build the first transcontinental railroad, 1877.

The Steel Industry

Steel is made out of iron, but it is stronger than ordinary iron. People used steel long before the Industrial Revolution, but it was very expensive to make. Then, in the middle 1800s, a man in England invented a cheap way to make iron into steel. At the same time, Americans discovered large amounts of iron near Lake Superior. This iron was made into steel in huge factories, and the steel was used to build bridges, railroads, and many other things. By 1900, the United States produced more steel than any other country.

The Oil Industry

Oil is found underground in many parts of the world. In the United States, oil was first found in 1859, in Pennsylvania. The Pennsylvania oil was first used to make the machines in factories run smoothly. Oils made from animals and plants were used before this, but the oil from the ground was cheaper and better. This oil also burned well, so people used it to light their houses. Later, people learned how to make oil into gasoline. They used the gasoline to run machines and cars. By 1900, oil was a big industry in the United States, and it still is.

UNDERSTANDING BAR GRAPHS

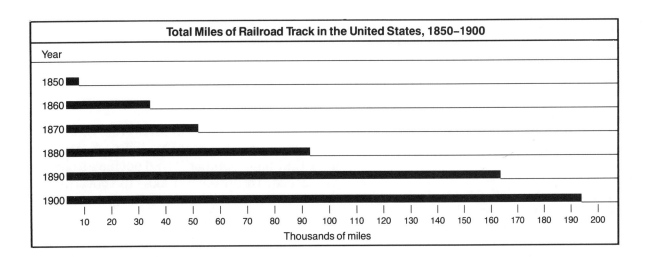

Total Miles of Railroad Track in the United States, 1850–1900

Study the bar graph and then answer the questions. Remember that the numbers at the bottom of the graph represent thousands of miles. This means that you should read 200 as "two hundred thousand miles."

1. The first railroad track in the United States were built in 1830. About how many thousands of miles of railroad track were built in total by 1850? _____

2. About how many thousand miles of railroad tracks were built by 1900? _____

3. By 1869, a railroad track crossed the United States from San Francisco, California to New York City. Look at the map on page 77. About how long was this railroad track? _____

4. About how many miles of <u>new</u> track were built between 1860 and 1870? _____

5. In which ten years were the most miles of <u>new</u> track built? Between _____ and _____

6. About how many miles of <u>new</u> track were built during those ten years? _____

Some Results of the Industrial Revolution

BEFORE YOU READ: Making Predictions

You have read about some of the new inventions and industries of the Industrial Revolution. How do you think these inventions and industries changed the lives of American people? Talk with a friend, a small group, or the class. List your ideas below.

_____

_____

_____

_____

_____

Now read the story below to learn about other changes the Industrial Revolution made in American life. See how many of your ideas are mentioned in the story.

Changes in American Life

The Industrial Revolution Brings Problems

The Industrial Revolution made many changes in the way people lived in the United States. Before the Industrial Revolution, most people lived on farms or in small towns. After the Industrial Revolution, more people moved to the cities where the factories were.

Work in the factories was hard. Many people worked for 12 to 14 hours every day, and they did not earn much money. Even children worked in the factories. In 1900, more than one out of every six children in the United States was a factory worker. Factory workers often got sick and died from the long, hard work.

Because the working conditions were so bad, some people got together to protect themselves. They formed groups called labor unions. Labor unions asked for better conditions and more pay for working people. They asked for laws to protect the children who worked in the factories. If they did not get what they asked for, the union members stopped working. When the factory owners tried to hire other workers, there was often violence.

Another problem caused by the Industrial Revolution was that some businesses became so large that small companies did not have a chance to succeed. In the early 1900s, the government made laws to limit the size of large businesses. These laws did not always work very well, however.

The Industrial Revolution Brings Improvements

The Industrial Revolution changed life in some good ways. One of the good changes was that many things became cheaper, and more people could buy them. Another good change was that the United States produced more things and sold them to other countries.

As the Industrial Revolution continued, inventors thought of more and more ways to make work easier or make life better. By 1900, people were using many of these inventions. People were using electric lights, telephones, and typewriters. They were listening to records of famous musicians. A few people were even driving around in automobiles. Life in America had certainly changed! In the years to come, it would change even more.

UNDERSTANDING WHAT YOU READ: Completing a Study Chart

Completing this study chart will help you recall important facts about the Industrial Revolution. You will find the facts you need on pages 80 and 81.

Look at the study chart below. Important dates in the Industrial Revolution are written in the left column. In the center column, you will write what happened on each date. In the right column, write why it was important. Write the important facts only. You do not have to write complete sentences. Remember, you will find the facts on pages 80 and 81.

Pennsylvania oil well, 1859

Date	What Happened	Why Important
late 1700s		
1790		
1830		
middle 1800s		
1859		
1869		

UNDERSTANDING WHAT YOU READ: Cause and Effect

1. Think about the reading on page 82. List at least two bad things that happened because of the Industrial Revolution.

_____

_____

_____

2. List at least two good things caused by the Industrial Revolution.

_____

_____

_____

Regions of the World: The Grasslands

In the second half of the 1800s, many pioneers moved west into the central part of the United States. After the pioneers crossed the Mississippi River, they entered a Grassland Region. First, they traveled on flat ground with high grass. This type of grassland is called a *prairie*. The prairie gets a lot of rain, from 20 to 35 inches a year. When the pioneers settled on the prairie, they planted crops of corn and wheat. This area became the best farmland in the United States.

As the pioneers traveled farther west, they came to the area that today we call the Great Plains. The Great Plains cover the western part of North Dakota, South Dakota, Nebraska, and Kansas, as well as the eastern part of Montana, Wyoming, and Colorado. This land was higher than the prairie. In the western part of the Great Plains the grass did not grow very high and there were no trees. This type of grassland is called a *steppe*. There is less rain on the steppe, only 10 to 20 inches a year. The steppe is a good region for raising animals that eat grass. Pioneers who settled on the Great Plains steppe built ranches and raised cattle and sheep. Farmers grew crops that needed less rain, such as wheat.

There are Grassland Regions in many parts of the world. There are prairies and steppes in many countries. A third type of grassland is called a *savannah*. A savannah is a tropical grassland, near the equator. The soil is not good in the savannah grasslands, so people do not farm. Instead they raise cattle, sheep, and goats, animals that eat the savannah grass.

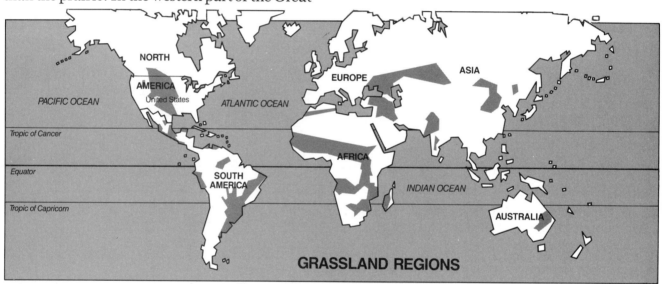

GRASSLAND REGIONS

UNDERSTANDING WHAT YOU READ: Using Maps

Look at the map. Answer these questions.

1. Which continents have Grassland Regions? _____

   _____

2. Which continents have savannahs? _____

3. List ten states that contain Grassland Regions. Look at the reading and the region map above, and the United States map on pages 6–7.

   _____

   _____

Cowboys and Cattle

BEFORE YOU READ: Focusing on What You Already Know

What do you already know about cowboys? Where did they live? What did they do?
Talk with a group of friends or with your class. List some facts you know about cowboys.

_____

_____

Now think of two things you'd like to know about cowboys. Write your two questions
below. Then as you read the story, see if you can find the answers to any of your questions.

_____

_____

The Cowboy

Cattle Ranching on the Great Plains

The steppe lands of the Great Plains were excellent for raising cattle, and some of the people who went west started ranches, or large farms, where they raised cattle and sold them for beef. People in the East wanted more beef, so the ranchers had no problem selling their cattle.

The Long Drive

When the cattle were ready to be sold, the ranchers sent them east by railroad. The ranchers hired cowboys to take the cattle from the ranch to the nearest "cow town," where the cattle were put into special railroad cars for the journey east.

The journey from the ranch to the cow town was called the "long drive." It was often many hundreds of miles to the railroad, and the long drive took several months.

The Life of a Cowboy

People today think cowboys' lives were glamorous and exciting. In fact, the cowboy's life was a hard one. He worked from sunrise until long after sunset every day during the long drive.

The cowboys rode horses. One of their main jobs was to see that cattle didn't run away from the herd. The youngest cowboy usually took care of the extra horses. Cowboys changed horses at least once a day.

The cattle spent the winter out on the grasslands. Each spring, the cowboys rode out on their horses, to find and "round up" the cattle. They brought them back into a "corral," an area with a fence around it. Young cattle had to be branded, that is, a special mark or "brand" was burned into their skin. Each ranch had its own brand. If cattle wandered away, the brand showed which ranch the cattle belonged to.

The first cowboys were Mexican Indians. After the Civil War, many soldiers became cowboys.

Cattle Ranching Changes

From 1879 to 1885 there were about 40,000 cowboys working in the West. After 1885, ranching changed. Farmers built fences to keep cattle off their land. The cattle were no longer able to wander free over the grasslands. Some ranchers started raising sheep instead of cattle. The railroads built more tracks to more places, so cattle could be put onto trains nearer the ranches. The long drives were not necessary anymore.

Ranches still use cowboys today, but they need only a few of them. Cattle go to the railroad on trucks. Some cowboys work on "dude ranches," where people from the cities go to spend a few weeks riding horses and having fun.

But the cowboys of a hundred years ago still live in books, movies, and TV programs, and in songs such as "Home on the Range."

UNDERSTANDING WHAT YOU READ: Using Context

Find the following vocabulary words in the story. Look at the words and sentences that come before and after the words. Decide what the words probably mean. Write your definitions on the lines below. If you wish, work with a friend.

1. beef _____

2. glamorous _____

3. sunrise _____

4. the herd _____

5. corral _____

   _____

6. wander _____

   _____

UNDERSTANDING WHAT YOU READ: Summarizing

1. List three jobs the cowboy did.

   _____

   _____

2. List three reasons cowboy life changed after 1885.

   _____

   _____

3. Did you find the answers to the questions you asked about cowboys on page 85? If so, write the answers below. If not, try to find the answer to at least one question in an encyclopedia or social studies book and write the answer below.

   _____

   _____

   _____

Native Americans: Treaties and Territories

"Indian Territory"

In the 1830s, the United States government forced the Cherokees, the Sauks, and other Indian tribes to leave their homelands in the East and move west of the Mississippi River into "Indian Territory." Indian Territory at this time included almost all the land between the Missouri River and the Oregon Territory.

Many Native American tribes had lived in this area for hundreds of years. The Sioux, the Cheyenne, and the Comanches were three Indian tribes who lived on the Great Plains. The Navajo, Apache, and Hopi were three tribes who lived in the deserts of the Southwest.

The Move to Reservations

The United States government signed treaties, or written agreements, with the Indian tribes promising that this land would belong to the Indians "as long as the rivers shall run and the grass shall grow." However, in the second half of the 1800s, railroad owners, pioneers, ranchers, and gold hunters all became very interested in this western land.

In the 1850s, the United States government began to buy parts of the Indian Territory from the Indian people and move the tribes to Indian reservations, special land set aside for Indian people. Reservations were usually set up on land that white settlers didn't want. The Indians were often forced to stay on these reservations.

Many Indian people did not want to sell their land. They did not want to live on reservations. They fought to save their homes, their hunting grounds, and their way of life.

The Buffalo of the Great Plains

The Indian people who lived on the Great Plains depended on the great buffalo herds for food, clothing, and tools. The pioneers and railroad men killed thousands of these buffalo for sport, for their fur, and to protect the new railroad tracks. In 1865 there were about 15 million buffalo on the Great Plains. Ten years later, only 1000 buffalo were left.

The death of the buffalo meant the end of the Plains Indians' way of life. There were terrible battles between the Indian tribes and United States soldiers. The Indians lost. Thousands of Native Americans were killed. The remaining members of the tribes were moved to Indian reservations.

The Sioux Indians of South Dakota

In 1874, gold was discovered in the Black Hills of South Dakota. The Black Hills belonged to the Sioux Indians. The United States government wanted to buy the land, but the Sioux did not want to sell. The United States army was sent to fight the Sioux and force them to leave the Black Hills and live on a reservation.

The Sioux Indians fought the United States army. In 1876, led by Chief Crazy Horse and Sitting Bull, the Sioux defeated General Custer and his forces in a battle. This battle became known as Custer's Last Stand. General Custer and all his men were killed. After this battle, however, new United States forces fought the Sioux Indians and defeated them. The Sioux were forced to move to a reservation. The Black Hills were taken over by gold miners and white settlers.

Indians of the Southwest Desert

In the Southwest, Native Americans were also forced to move to reservations. Many Indians disliked reservation life and fought to live as they had in the past. One of the most famous fighters was Geronimo, an Apache chief. From 1876 to 1886, Geronimo and his Apache warriors attacked U.S. settlements and soldiers. Many men, women, and children were killed before the Apache surrendered and returned to the reservation.

Chief Geronimo and his wife.

Indian Reservations Today

Today, more than 250 different Indian tribes have reservations. Life on the reservations is not always easy, and many young Indians choose to leave the reservation and live and work in the cities. Some reservations have set up businesses that make money to support the people who live on the reservation. For example, a business on a Cherokee reservation makes computer parts. Other businesses on reservations include factories, ski resorts, and vacation hotels.

Many Native Americans still speak the language of their tribe. They believe it is important to keep the tribal culture alive. They want their children to remember and appreciate the Indian way of life.

ACTIVITY: Interviewing Native Americans

Do you know any Native American Indians or people who are partly Native Americans? If you do, please talk to them or telephone them and find answers to these questions.

1. What is the name of their tribe?

_____

2. Where was the first home of this tribe?

_____

3. Do they know any Indian language? If so, what is the name of the language?

_____

Sitting Bull

LISTENING AND TAKING NOTES

You are going to listen to some information about Sitting Bull, an important leader of the Sioux Indians. As you listen, take notes on the information using the *T-List* below. The main ideas are written on the left. Write the details and examples on the right.

MAIN IDEAS	DETAILS AND EXAMPLES
A. Who was Sitting Bull?	
B. Sitting Bull prepares the Sioux for battle (Custer's Last Stand)	
C. After Custer's Last Stand	
D. How Sitting Bull died	
E. Why Sitting Bull is important	

Regions of the World: The Deserts

The largest Indian reservation in the United States is the Navajo reservation in parts of Arizona, New Mexico, and Utah. This reservation is in the Desert Region of the southwestern United States. The Hopi, Apache, and Zuni tribes also have reservations in the southwestern Desert Region.

Desert Regions are the driest regions on earth. It is difficult for people to live in Desert Regions because very little rain falls in the desert.

Since deserts are so dry, there are not many plants or animals in them. Very few plants can grow in a desert because there is not enough water for them. Plants that do grow in deserts have special ways to get water. Some desert plants have long roots that go deep into the ground to find water. Other desert plants, such as the cactus, store water in their leaves so that they can live when there is no rain.

The animals and birds that live in the desert also have special ways to find water and food.

The highest temperatures in the world are in Desert Regions. This means that in the daytime, deserts are usually very hot. The sun shines brightly, there are few clouds, the air is dry, and there are no large trees to give shade. Deserts can also be very cold at night. The desert air is very dry, so the heat of the day disappears when the sun goes down.

In some deserts, people have made irrigation systems that bring water from far away. In Arizona and New Mexico, for example, there are many dams on rivers. Water collects behind the dams. This water is then taken to desert areas so that farmers can grow crops.

Although deserts do not have much water, they do have other natural resources. The world's richest oil fields are in desert areas. In Desert Regions of the southwestern part of the United States, there are minerals such as copper, gold, silver, and uranium.

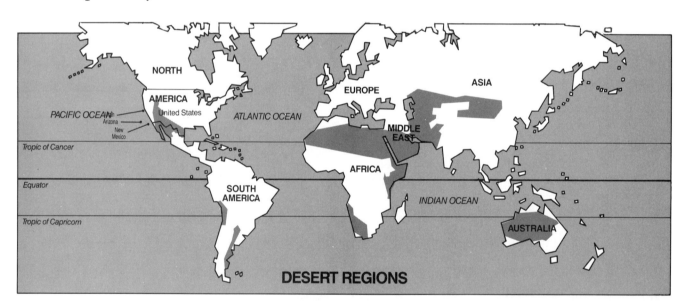

DESERT REGIONS

USING MAPS

Look at the map of Desert Regions and answer these questions.

1. Where is the largest Desert Region in the world? _____

2. Which continent does not have a Desert Region? _____

3. In what part of the United States are Desert Regions found? _____

ACTIVITY: What Do You Think?

Could you live in a desert? Think of the things you would need in a desert. On the lines below, write a list of the ten most important things you would need to live in a desert.

1. _____   6. _____

2. _____   7. _____

3. _____   8. _____

4. _____   9. _____

5. _____   10. _____

Now sit in a group with four or five classmates. Compare your lists. Talk about the reasons why you chose each thing on your list. Listen to your classmates. Write two good ideas that your classmates had.

1. _____

2. _____

With your classmates, talk about the five most important things that you would need to live in the desert. Talk about this until everyone in your group agrees on five important things. Then write these five things on the lines and give a good reason why each thing is necessary.

1. _____ is important because _____

   _____ .

2. Do not forget to take _____ to the desert because

   _____ .

3. If you want to _____ ,

   you should take _____ the desert.

4. My friends and I think that it is important to have _____

   in the desert because _____ .

5. Finally, don't ever forget to take _____ to the

   desert because _____ .

Inventions in the United States: 1792–1903

Read the information on the chart and be sure you understand how each invention is used. All these inventions were made in the United States. There were also important inventions in other countries.

Date	Invention	Inventor	Explanation
1792	**Cotton Gin**	Eli Whitney	Takes seeds out of cotton. One person could do same work as 50 people picking out seeds by hand. Farmers could produce more cotton.
1834	**Reaper**	Cyrus McCormick	Horse-drawn machine cuts grain, such as wheat. Farmers in West could plant more wheat.
1844	**Telegraph**	Samuel F. B. Morse	Sends messages through wires, using a code for each letter of the alphabet. By 1850s, telegraph wires all over United States. People could communicate over long distances quickly.
1846	**Sewing Machine**	Elias Howe	Sews faster than by hand. Helped people to make clothes for their families more rapidly. Led to factories that made clothes (including uniforms for soldiers and sailors); early factories had bad working conditions.
1867	**Typewriter**	Christopher L. Sholes	Writes faster than by hand. Changed the way people in offices worked. Many women found office jobs as typists.
1876	**Telephone**	Alexander Graham Bell	Sends spoken messages through wires. People could communicate by voice over long distances.
1877	**Phonograph (Record Player)**	Thomas A. Edison	Makes a permanent record of sounds. People could hear music and speech that had been played, sung, or spoken earlier, and they could hear it as often as they wished to.
1879	**Electric Light Bulb**	Thomas A. Edison	Makes light from electricity. People could use electricity for light in their homes instead of candles, gas lights, or oil lamps. Electricity provided more light and was clean.

| 1888 | **Kodak Camera** | George Eastman | Takes a photograph. First simple camera that anyone could use. People could take pictures of family, friends, pets, etc. |
| 1903 | **Airplane** | Wilbur and Orville Wright | Transports people and things through the air. First flight of powered airplane at Kitty Hawk, North Carolina, December 17, 1903. Makes travel much faster. |

UNDERSTANDING WHAT YOU READ: Study Questions

Write five questions about inventions in the United States. Use the question words *when, what, who,* and *why.* Here are some examples of questions:

When was the telephone invented?
What invention can take a photograph?

Who invented the telegraph?
Why was the cotton gin important?

1. _____ ?

2. _____ ?

3. _____ ?

4. _____ ?

5. _____ ?

Now sit in groups of four to five classmates. Take turns asking questions to the people in your group. When all the questions have been asked and answered, discuss the questions. Which were easy? Which were difficult? Write the two most difficult questions and their answers on the lines below.

Question: _____

Answer: _____

Question: _____

Answer: _____

ACTIVITY: Learn About Another Invention

Find out about some inventions that have been made since 1903. Your teacher or school librarian can help you find the information you need. Write about one of these inventions on your paper. Tell who invented it, when it was invented, and how it changed people's lives.

Reforms and Reformers

Factory Life: Francis Cabot Lowell

Francis Cabot Lowell was one of the early factory owners in the United States. Lowell believed that factory work did not have to be unpleasant. He built a city along the Merrimack River in Massachusetts. His city had factories for making cloth, but it also had good houses for the workers. It had schools and churches too. The city was named Lowell for the man who started it.

Francis Cabot Lowell hired young women from the farms near his city. He paid them more than they could earn on the farm. They lived in comfortable houses. Lowell encouraged the women to eat good food and to continue their schooling. The "Lowell Girls," as they were called, were famous all over the United States.

Most factory workers were not as lucky as the "Lowell Girls." They were badly paid. They worked very long hours. The factories were noisy and unhealthy. People who complained were fired. More and more children worked in the factories.

"Lowell Girls."

Jane Addams at Hull House.

Help for the Poor: Jane Addams

In the last part of the 1800s, many men and women tried to help factory workers and other poor people. We call these men and women "reformers," because of the reforms, or changes, they tried to make. One of these people was Jane Addams.

Jane Addams was born in 1860. Her family was rich, but she wanted to help poor people. She visited a "settlement house" in London, a place where poor people could play and learn. In 1889, she started a settlement house in Chicago. She called it Hull House.

Hull House was in a very poor neighborhood. It gave classes in art, music, and crafts. It helped people learn to read better. It took care of children during the days, and it had a gymnasium where people could exercise. Hull House also helped immigrants learn about the United States and get ready to become citizens.

Words and Pictures: Jacob Riis

Jacob Riis helped the poor in a different way. In 1890, Riis wrote a book called *How the Other Half Lives.* In it, he told about life in the tenements, or poor apartment houses, in New York City. He also took photographs of these apartments and of the people who lived in them. His books and pictures made people understand what life was like for poor people in the cities.

Photo by Jacob Riis.

Photo by Jacob Riis.

Other Reforms: Laws

At the same time that Jane Addams and Jacob Riis were active, other reforms were going on in the United States. Many states passed laws to make factories safer and cleaner. Other laws made sure that food was pure.

Many states also passed laws to stop, or at least to limit, the hiring of children. Today, children are allowed to do farm work or to work for their parents. But they no longer can work in factories.

In 1900, more than one out of every six children in the United States worked in a factory or mine.

The young girl (above right) worked in a textile factory.

The "breaker boys" (right) worked in a coal mine, separating pieces of coal from slate. They often worked 10 hours a day.

The Age of Industry   **95**

Thirteen Presidents: 1850–1900

Thirteen men served as President of the United States between 1850 and 1900.
Listed below are some things that happened while they were President.

	President	Events
–1850	Millard Fillmore	1850– President Zachary Taylor dies July 9; Fillmore becomes President.
–		
–		1852– *Uncle Tom's Cabin*, by Harriet Beecher Stowe, published.
–	Franklin Pierce	1853– Gadsden Purchase.
–		
–1855		
–		1856– John Brown kills 5 proslavery settlers at Pottawatomie Creek, KS.
–	James Buchanan	
–		
–		1859– John Brown attacks Harper's Ferry, Virginia; is tried and hanged.
–1860	Abraham Lincoln	1861– 11 states secede from the Union; the Civil War begins.
–		
–		1863– { West Virginia admitted to the Union. / Emancipation Proclamation frees slaves in Confederate states.
–		
–1865	Andrew Johnson	1865– Civil War ends; Lincoln killed; 13th Amendment abolishes slavery.
–		1867– United States buys Alaska from Russia for $7,200,000.
–		1868– { 14th Amendment gives citizenship to blacks; Congress tries to remove President Johnson; fails by one vote.
–	Ulysses S. Grant	1869– Wyoming gives vote to women; transcontinental RR completed.
–1870		1870– 15th Amendment guarantees voting rights for black American men.
–		
–		1872– Vice-President Colfax accused of corruption.
–		1873– *The Gilded Age*, by Mark Twain and Charles Warner, published.
–		
–1875		1876– { General Custer attacks Sioux in Montana; he and 264 soldiers killed; first telephone lines between cities.
–	Rutherford B. Hayes	1877– Thomas A. Edison invents phonograph (record player).
–		
–		1879– Thomas A. Edison invents electric light bulb.
–1880		
–	James A. Garfield (Mar. 4)	1881– President Garfield shot July 2, dies September 19.
–	Chester A. Arthur (Sept. 20)	1882– Chinese Exclusion Act forbids immigration of Chinese.
–		1883– Congress sets up system of written tests for government jobs.
–		
–1885	Grover Cleveland	
–		
–		1887– Statue of Liberty completed in New York Harbor.
–	Benjamin Harrison	1889– Jane Addams opens Hull House in Chicago.
–		
–1890		1890– { Sherman Antitrust Act to regulate big businesses. / Jacob Riis publishes *How the Other Half Lives*.
–		
–	Grover Cleveland	
–		1894– First showing of motion pictures (movies).
–1895		
–		
–	William McKinley	
–		1898– { Spanish-American War: U.S. acquires Puerto Rico, Guam, Philippines. United States annexes independent republic of Hawaii.
–		
–1900		

UNDERSTANDING TIME LINES: Comprehension Check

Use the time line on page 96 to answer these questions.

1. The Constitution says that if a President dies during his term of office, the Vice-President becomes President. What three Vice-Presidents became President in this way between 1850 and 1900, and when did they become President?

   _____   _____   _____

2. Which President served less than one year? _____

3. What happened in the same year that the transcontinental railroad was completed?

   _____

4. Which came first, the telephone or the electric light bulb? _____

5. Many Presidents have served two terms, but only one served two terms that did not immediately follow each other. Who was this President? _____

6. Under what President was a system of written tests set up for government jobs?

   _____

7. Who was President when the United States acquired Alaska? _____

8. Who owned Alaska before the United States bought it? _____

9. Impeachment by Congress is the first step in legally removing a President. Who is the only President ever to have been impeached? _____

10. Who was President when the United States went to war against Spain? _____

WHAT DO YOU THINK?

Imagine it is 1899. You live on a farm. You have just learned that your area is going to get electricity and telephone service next year. You've never seen electric lights or telephones, but you have read about them in newspapers and magazines.

Talk with a group of friends. How do you think these new inventions will change your life? Write your ideas below.

_____

_____

_____

Immigrants in the United States

BEFORE YOU READ: Using Section Headings

Look at the five section headings in the reading below and on page 99. Then read the questions below. In which section do you think you would find the answer to these questions? Write the subtitle on the line. Then skim the section to find the answer to the questions. Write the answer on the line. You do not have to write complete sentences.

1. Where do most United States immigrants come from today?

   Section Heading: _____

   Answer: _____

2. Where did most immigrants in the 1700s come from?

   Section Heading: _____

   Answer: _____

3. When were the first ESL classes started in public schools?

   Section Heading: _____

   Answer: _____

4. Are all Americans from immigrant families?

   Section Heading: _____

   Answer: _____

5. What sorts of jobs did United States immigrants get in the 1800s?

   Section Heading: _____

   Answer: _____

Now read the story to find out more information about immigrants in the United States.

Immigration to the United States

A Nation of Immigrants

Immigrants are people who come into a new country to settle and live. The United States has always been a nation of immigrants. Except for Native American Indians, everyone's family has come to the United States from another country at some time during the last three or four hundred years. Even the American Indians immigrated to the Americas from Asia many thousands of years ago.

Early Immigrants

In the 1600s and early 1700s, most immigrants came from Europe. Settlers immigrated from Spain to what is now the southwestern part of the United States. Other immigrants from England and other northern and western European countries settled on the east coast of North America.

Descendents of these east-coast people fought for independence from England. They built the new nation, the United States of America.

After the Civil War, many more people immigrated to the United States. There were three main reasons why so many immigrants came in the late 1800s. First, many people wanted religious freedom. This was the same reason that brought immigrants to Plymouth, Massachusetts, in 1620. Second, many people wanted to live in a democratic country so that they could have freedom. Third, the crops in Europe were bad and there was not enough food, so people came to the United States.

How Immigrants Survived

Life in the United States was not easy for most immigrants. Many immigrants were well educated in their own language, but they did not know English. Other immigrants had very little education and few skills. They all had to find jobs in order to survive.

Thousands of immigrants came from Ireland, Italy, Russia, Poland, and other countries in southern and eastern Europe. They settled in large cities in the Northeast and worked in factories. Factory work was hard, the hours were long, and the pay was low.

Many Chinese immigrants arrived in California. They helped to build railroads and bridges in the western part of the country. Later, many Chinese became farm workers. Immigrants from Germany, Norway, and Sweden settled on the Great Plains and became farmers and business people.

Chinatown, San Francisco, California.

Immigrants and Public Schools

Public schools in the United States helped immigrants in many ways. First, the schools gave children a free education. This meant that many young people became better educated than their parents and had more chances for better jobs. In addition, many schools had evening classes for adults.

One of the important jobs of the schools was to teach English. At first, the school put immigrant children in classes with much younger English-speaking children until the immigrant children learned English. Some schools had bilingual classes in which students could study in their first language as well as in English.

In 1904, some schools started special language classes for children who did not speak English. These were the first English as a Second Language (ESL) classes in the United States. Today there are bilingual classes and ESL classes in many public schools.

ESL class in New York City, 1910.

ESL students today.

Recent Immigrants

Immigration continues in the United States today. Every year, thousands of new Americans settle in different parts of the country. They come because of war, because of hunger, or because they want religious or political freedom. The largest group of recent immigrants has come from countries in Southeast Asia such as Vietnam, Cambodia, and Laos. Another large group comes from Spanish-speaking countries in Central America and South America.

Most of these people have the same kinds of difficulties in finding jobs and getting an education that earlier immigrants had. Like these earlier immigrants, today's immigrants hope that they can make a better life for themselves and their children.

UNDERSTANDING WHAT YOU READ: Writing Study Questions

Work with a partner. For each section of the reading, write one or two questions that will help you study and remember the main information in that section.

_____

_____

_____

_____

_____

_____

_____

Now work by yourself. Write answers to your study questions. You do not have to write complete sentences. You may need to use some extra paper.

_____
_____
_____
_____
_____
_____
_____
_____
_____
_____
_____
_____
_____
_____
_____
_____
_____
_____
_____

ACTIVITY: Study Quiz

Ask your partner three of the study questions above. Your partner has to answer without looking at the book. Then your partner will ask you three study questions. How well do you remember the information?

Developing Reports: Your Family Story

MAKING A FAMILY TREE

Everyone in the United States comes from an immigrant family. Some families were immigrants many years ago. Other families were immigrants a short time ago. What about your family? Complete the family tree below. Write in the names of your family members and the country where each person was born. Ask your parents or another family member to help you.

MY FAMILY TREE

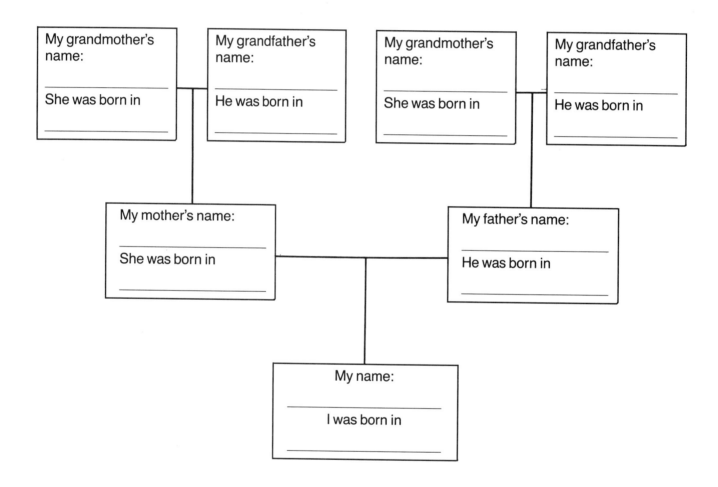

RESEARCHING AND WRITING

Now you will write a story about how your family came to the United States. (You can write a story about another family if you prefer.) First you will make notes on the important things in your family's immigration story. Second, you will write the story on a separate piece of paper. Third, you will work with a friend to make your story better. Fourth, you will write your revised story on page 104. Fifth, you will read your story to a group of classmates and listen to their family stories. Finally, you will discuss ways in which some of your family stories are alike.

1. Notes on your family story

Where my family lived before they came to the United States:

_____

How my family lived in their country:

_____

_____

Why my family left their country:

_____

_____

How my family came to the United States:

_____

_____

What happened when my family arrived in the United States:

_____

_____

Problems my family has had in the United States and how we have solved them:

_____

_____

_____

2. First draft of your family story

Write your first draft on a separate piece of paper. First, organize your ideas. Decide on the most important ideas and which ideas come first, second, third, etc. Write an introductory paragraph that tells what your story is about. In the main body of your story, write the important ideas and some details or examples that explain the ideas. You will probably have three or four paragraphs in the main body of your story. Finally, write a concluding paragraph which tells the most important things in your story.

3. Work with a friend

Now ask a friend to read your story and make comments. Can your friend understand your story? Can your friend see what the main ideas are? Does your friend think that the order you used for your different ideas is the best order? Does your friend see any mistakes in spelling, grammar, or punctuation?

4. Rewrite your story

After working with your friend, rewrite your story. Write the final draft of your story on page 104.

MY FAMILY STORY

PRESENTING AN ORAL REPORT

Sit in a small group with three other classmates. Read your stories to one another.
Be ready to anwer questions after reading your story. Now write three important
things that you learned from listening to each classmate's story.

LISTENING AND TAKING NOTES

_____ 's Family Story

_____

_____

_____

_____ 's Family Story

_____

_____

_____

_____ 's Family Story

_____

_____

_____

COMPARING FAMILY STORIES

With your group, talk about ways in which some of your family stories are alike.
List some of these similarities below.

_____

_____

_____

_____

_____

A. Circle the letter of the best answer.

1. The United States acquired Puerto Rico as a result of the:
   a. annexation of Hawaii   **b.** Spanish-American War   **c.** War of 1812
   d. Mexican War

2. Which of the following is NOT related to the Industrial Revolution in America?
   a. how things were made   **b.** how products were carried from farms and plantations
   c. how the United States government worked   **d.** the kind of work people did

3. Labor unions were started because:
   a. many people stopped working   **b.** many things became cheaper
   c. most people worked on farms   **d.** working conditions were bad

4. In what part of the United States is most of the grassland region?
   a. the central part   **b.** the West Coast   **c.** the East Coast   **d.** the South

5. Which of these Native American Indian tribes did NOT live on the Great Plains before the 1830s?
   a. Cherokee   **b.** Sioux   **c.** Cheyenne   **d.** Comanche

6. Irrigation systems are used to:
   a. make iron into steel   **b.** help machines to run smoothly
   c. bring water to grow crops   **d.** build bridges and railroads

7. The telephone was invented by:
   a. Alexander Bell   **b.** Thomas Edison   **c.** Samuel Morse   **d.** George Eastman

8. The "Lowell Girls" were:
   a. women who tried to help poor people   **b.** women who refused to work
   c. women who stayed on the farm   **d.** women who made cloth in factories

9. In what way is Grover Cleveland different from all other Presidents of the United States?
   a. He served two terms, several years apart.   **b.** He was impeached by Congress.
   c. His Vice-President was accused of taking bribes.   **d.** His term lasted only one month.

10. Most immigrants today come from:
    a. England and western Europe
    b. Southeast Asia, Central America, and South America
    c. Ireland, Italy, Russia, and Poland   **d.** northern Europe, Spain, and China

B. Match each person's name with the correct description.

1. Jane Addams ____   **a.** made a fortune in the oil industry

2. Andrew Carnegie ____   **b.** attacked Sioux in South Dakota and was killed by them

3. John D. Rockefeller ____   **c.** invented a machine to take seeds out of cotton

4. Eli Whitney ____   **d.** started a "settlement house" in Chicago

5. George A. Custer ____   **e.** made a fortune in the steel industry

6. Jacob Riis ____   **f.** took photographs and wrote books about poor people in cities

C. Write one or two sentences about each of these American inventions. Tell what it did and how it changed the lives of Americans.

1. reaper _____

_____

2. sewing machine _____

_____

3. phonograph _____

_____

4. Kodak camera _____

_____

D. What Do You Think?

Discuss these questions with a friend, a small group, or the class. These are "thought questions." They do not have simple right or wrong anwers.

1. At various times, the United States Congress has passed laws to limit the number of immigrants allowed to come to the United States. Some of these laws have limited the number of immigrants from particular parts of the world. Why do you think Congress passed these laws? Do you think laws like these are necessary? Why or why not?

2. When the Industrial Revolution began in England, people destroyed many factories and machines. When the Industrial Revolution came to the United States, people were glad to take jobs in factories. Why do you think English workers acted the way they did? Why do you think American workers did not act this way? How do you think you would have acted if you had been living in the United States when the Industrial Revolution started?

E. Role-Play

Work with a partner. Make up conversations that might have taken place in one or both of these situations. Think about what you will say, but do not write it down. Listen to what your partner says, so that you will be able to answer him or her. Try to "be" the person whose role you are playing.

1. It is 1888. One of you is a factory owner. The other is a reformer who wants to stop the factory from hiring children.

2. It is 1900. One of you is a factory owner. The other is a worker who has recently immigrated to the United States from a country in southern or eastern Europe. The worker is complaining about bad conditions, long hours, and low pay.

Glossary

The words in this glossary have been defined according to the way they are used in this book. You may want to check your dictionary for other meanings. The pronunciation key is from *Thorndike-Barnhart Intermediate Dictionary*, by E.L. Thorndike and Clarence L. Barnhart. Copyright © 1974 Scott, Foresman and Company. Reprinted by permission.

a	hat, cap	f	fat, if	n	no, in	s	say, yes	w	will, woman
ā	age, face	g	go, bag	ng	long, bring	sh	she, rush	y	young, yet
ä	father, far	h	he, how			t	tell, it	z	zero, breeze
				o	hot, rock	th	thin, both	zh	measure, seizure
b	bad, rob	i	it, pin	ō	open, go	TH	then, smooth		
ch	child, much	ī	ice, live	ȯ	order, all			ə	represents:
d	did, red			oi	oil, voice	u	cup, butter		a in about
		j	jam, enjoy	ou	house, out	u̇	full, put		e in taken
e	let, best	k	kind, seek			ü	rule, move		i in pencil
ē	equal, be	l	land, coal	p	paper, cup				o in lemon
ėr	term, learn	m	me, am	r	run, try	v	very, save		u in circus

abolish (ə·bäl′ish) To stop or put an end to something.

abolitionist (ab′ə·lish′ən ·ist) A person who wanted to abolish, or put an end to slavery.

acquire (ə·kwīr′) To get or become the owner of something.

admit (əd·mit′) To allow something or someone to come in.

agriculture (ag′ri·kul′ cher) Farming.

almanac (ȯl′mə·nak) A book published each year which contains information about many different subjects.

amendment (ə·mend′mənt) A section that is added to a document to change or improve it.

annex (ə·neks′) To add a territory to a country without fighting for it or buying it.

apart (ə·part′) Away from or separated from something.

apartment (ə·pärt′mənt) A room or rooms in a house for people to live in.

approve (ə·prüv′) To say something is good, to agree with.

architect (är′kə·tekt) A person who designs buildings.

armory (är′mə·rē) A building where a government keeps guns and other weapons.

atlas (at′ləs) A book of maps.

brand (brand) A mark burned on the skin of an animal to show who owns the animal.

boundary (boun′drē) A line showing the border or edge of a state or country.

bribe (brīb) Money paid to a person to do something wrong or against the law.

buffalo (buf′ə·lo) A large animal related to the cow, that once lived on the Great Plains of North America.

bureau (byu′rō) A government department for giving information to people and helping them.

canal (cə·nal′) A waterway like a river but made by people.

candidate (kan′də·dāt′) A person who tries to get elected.

cannery (kan′ər·ē) A factory that puts food into cans.

capture (kap′chər) To take and hold as a prisoner, to catch an animal.

cattle (kat′l) Cows and bulls.

cession (sesh′ən) Giving up something to someone else.

charity (char′ə·tē) Love and good will.

civil war (siv′l wor) A war between two groups of people in the same country.

claim (klām) 1. To say that something belongs to you or to your country, etc.: to *claim* the land for Spain.
2. Something a person or country says it owns.

climate (klī′mət) The kind of weather that a place generally has.

coast (kōst) The land next to the ocean or sea.

compare (kəm·per′) To tell how two things are the same.

compromise (kom′prə·mīz′) An agreement to settle an argument. In a *compromise*, each side gives up some of what it wants.

conceive (kən·sēv′) To think up or begin something.

Confederacy (kən·fed′ər·ə·sē) A name for the states that seceded from the United States in 1860 and 1861.

contrast (kən·trast′) To tell how two things are different.

contribution (kän′trəbyü′shən) Something that someone gives to other people.

corral (kə·ral′) A fenced area to hold cattle.

corruption (kə·rup′shən) Behavior that is not honest.

cow town (kou′ toun) A city or town where cattle were put into railroad cars after the "long drive."

crops (kräps) Plants grown for food or money.

culture (kul′chər) The entire way of life of a particular people, their customs, language, tools, etc.

dam (dam) A wall or barrier to hold back water in a river.

defeat (di·fēt′) To beat someone in a battle or war.

degree (di·grē′) 1. A unit used to measure temperature.
2. A unit used to measure latitude.

demand (di·mand′) 1. To make a request that must be met.
2. This kind of request.

desert (dez′ert) A dry region often covered with sand.

disease (di·zēz′) A sickness or illness.

disobey (dis·ə·bā′) Not to do as you are told.

doctrine (däk′trən) A statement that tells what you believe in, a rule or principle to follow.

double (dub′l) To become two times as big.

dude ranch (dyüd′ ranch) A place where people go to ride horses and have fun.

encyclopedia (in·sī′klə·pe′·dē·ə) A set of books with information on many different things.

equator (i·kwāt′ər) An imaginary line around the earth, halfway between the North Pole and the South Pole.

establish (ə·stab′lish) To set up or found.

exist (ig·zist′) To be.

farmland (färm′land) Land used for growing crops and raising cows, sheep, etc.

fire (fīr) 1. To shoot a gun. 2. To tell someone that he or she cannot work for you anymore.

force (fȯrs) 1. To make someone do something. 2. Power you use to make someone do something or make something happen.

foreign (fȯr′in) Connected to other countries.

foreign policy (fȯr′in päl′ə·sē) A set of rules and customs for dealing with other countries.

fortune (fȯr′chən) A very large amount of money.

frontier (frun·tir′) The edge of settled land.

gap (gap) 1. A low place in a range of mountains. 2. A difference between things.

gild (gild) To put a thin layer of gold on something.

glamorous (glam′ər·əs) Attractive, exciting, filled with pleasure.

goods (gu̇dz) Things that are made by people to sell.

greed (grēd) Wanting more than you need or deserve to have.

guide (gīd) A person who points out the way.

guilty (gil′tē) Having done something wrong.

harvest (här′vist) 1. To gather and bring in a crop. 2. The crops gathered in one season.

hemisphere (hem′ə·sfir′) One-half of the earth's surface: the northern and southern *hemispheres*.

herd (herd) 1. A large group of one kind of large animal, such as cattle. 2. To control a large group of cattle or other large animals from horseback.

hero (hir′ō) A person who does something brave to save other people or to help his or her country.

homeland (hōm′land) The country where you were born or where your home is.

immigrant (im′ə·grənt) A person who comes into a new country to settle and live.

impeach (im·pēch′) To take the first step in removing a President by accusing the President of doing things that are against the law.

income (in′kum) The money that people or companies get from the work they do.

industrial (in·dus′tre·əl) Connected with businesses or companies.

industry (in′dəs·trē) All the businesses or companies that make a particular thing or provide a particular service: the steel *industry*, the railroad *industry*.

injustice (in·jus′tis) Unfairness, not being just or fair.

intangible (in·tan′jə·bəl) Something that cannot be touched, handled, or seen.

interfere (in·tər·fir′) To try to tell others what to do when they don't want you to.

invention (in·ven′shən) Something that is made or thought up for the first time.

inventor (in·ven′tər) Someone who builds something entirely new or different; someone who makes or thinks up something for the first time.

iron (ī′ərn) A hard metal that is found in the ground.

irrigation (ir′rə·gā′shən) Bringing water to an area from far away so that farmers can grow crops.

journey (jėr′nē) A trip from one place to another.

jury (ju̇′rē) A group of people who decide if a person did or did not do something wrong.

latitude (lat′ə·tüd) The distance north or south of the equator. *Latitude* lines are imaginary lines around the earth that run east-west on the globe.

lecturer (lek′chər·ər) A person who gives talks or speeches to groups of people.

log (log) A part of a tree that has been cut down.

log cabin (log kab′n) A small house made of logs.

lumber (lum′bər) Trees that have been cut into boards.

malice (mal′is) A desire to hurt someone.

manufacturing (man′yə·fak′chər·ing) Making something in a factory.

miner (mī′nər) A person who digs minerals out of the earth.

mineral (min′ər·əl) A substance such as coal or gold found in the earth that people put to use.

movement (müv′mənt) 1. A series of activities by people working together to make changes or reach a goal: Susan B. Anthony was leader in the *movement* for women's rights. 2. A motion or action.

national anthem (nash′ə·nəl an′thəm) The official song of a country.

obey (ō·bā′) To do as you are told.

oil field (oil′ fēld) A place where much oil is found under the ground.

operate (äp′ər·āt) To work a machine.

pardon (pär′dən) To forgive.

path (path) A narrow place to walk through wild land.

phonograph (fō′nə·graf) A machine to play records.

pioneer (pī·ə·nir′) Someone who does something before most other people do it, one of the first people to settle in a new area.

plains (plānz) Large areas of flat land.

plantation (plan·tā′shən) A very large farm where only one crop is grown.

plow (plou) A large tool used to break up soil for planting.

population (pop′yə·la′shən) The number of people in a place such as a city, state, or country.

poverty (päv′ər·tē) Poorness, having little or no property.

product (präd′əkt) Something that is made or grown.

proposition (präp′ə·zi′shən) An idea or plan.

ranch (ranch) A large farm for raising cattle, horses, or sheep.

rancher (ran′cher) A person who owns a ranch.

rare (rer) Not common, not often found, unusual.

ratify (rat′ə.fı′) To approve something such as a law, by voting.

readmit (rē′əd.mit′) Allow someone or something to come in again.

reaper (rē′pər) A machine for harvesting a crop of grain.

rebuild (rē.bild′) To build something again.

Reconstruction (rē′kən.struk′shən) The rebuilding of the South after the Civil War, from 1865 to 1877.

reformer (ri.for′mer) A person who tries to help poor people, anyone who tries to improve the world.

regain (ri.gān′) To get back something you used to have.

relations (ri.lā′shənz) Connections or dealings between people or between groups such as countries.

removal (ri.müv′əl) Taking something or someone away from a place, job. etc.

rent (rent) A payment made to the owner of property for the use of that property for a period of time.

repeal (ri.pēl′) To cancel or do away with a law.

reservation (rez′ər.vā′shən) Land that is kept for a particular use. There are many Indian *reservations* in the United States.

resort (ri.zȯrt′) A place where people go to enjoy themselves.

reunite (rē′yü.nit′) To put back together again.

revolt (ri.vōlt′) To fight against the government.

revolution (rev′ə.lü′shən) A war that is fought to overthrow the ruling government.

revolve (ri.volv′) To spin or turn around.

road (rōd) A way made for traveling between places using horses, wagons, or autmobiles, etc.

route (rüt) A road or path between two or more places.

rush (rush) A movement of many people to get to a place. In 1849 there was a gold *rush* to California.

savannah (sə.van′ə) A tropical grassland near the equator used for raising cattle, sheep, and goats.

score (skȯr) Twenty.

secede (si.sēd′) To stop being part of a country, state, etc. When Lincoln was elected, eleven states *seceded*.

secession (si.sesh′ən) Seceding or separating from a country, state, etc.

segregate (seg′rə.gāt′) To separate one group of people from others. After Reconstruction, laws *segregated* blacks, that is, separated them from whites.

settlement house (set′əl.mənt hous) A place where poor people can play and learn.

sharecropper (sher′cräp.ər) A person who rents land and gives a share of the crops to the owner as rent.

skill (skil) An ability to do a job.

slavery (slā′və.rē) A system in which one person can own another person.

steel (stēl) A metal that is made out of iron but is stronger than ordinary iron.

steppe (step) A grassland with short grass, no trees, and 10 to 20 inches of rainfall in a year.

stretch (strech) To cover or continue over a space. The Rocky Mountains *stretch* from Canada to Mexico.

suffrage (suf′rij) The right to vote.

suited to (süt′əd tü) Good for a particular use or purpose.

survive (sėr.vīv′) To go through hard times and come out alive, to stay alive.

tangible (tan′jib.əl) Something that can be touched, handled, or seen.

tariff (tar′if) A tax on goods that come into a country from other countries.

tenement (ten′ə.mənt) An apartment where poor people live.

term (tėrm) A period of time, the period of time for which a President of the United States is elected.

textile (tex′tīl) Cloth.

thread (thred) A long piece of cotton, silk, or other material made by spinning. Cloth is made out of *thread* by weaving.

tourist (tür′ist) A person who travels for pleasure.

trail (trāl) A path or way marked in some way so that others can follow it.

train (trān) A set of railroad cars pulled by a locomotive.

treason (trēz′ən) Going against your country, giving secret information about your country to another country.

treaties (trē′tēz) Written agreements between countries.

trial (tri′əl) The way that a court finds out if a person has broken the law or if a claim is correct.

tribe (trib) A group of families living together, sharing a culture, and having one chief or leader.

troops (trüps) Soldiers.

unequal (un.ē′kwəl) Not the same, in amount, size, or treatment, for example.

union (yün′yən) A group of workers who get together to protect themselves against bad working conditions, low pay, etc.

Union (yün′yən) A name for the United States of America.

unite (yü.nit′) To put together, to make one thing out of two or more things.

veto (vē′tō) To stop a law by not signing it. The President can *veto* a law passed by Congress.

violence (vī′ə.ləns) The use of force or power to damage or destroy something or kill somebody.

wander (wän′dər) To walk away.

wealthy (wel′thē) Rich, having lots of money or property.

world power (wėrld pou′ər) A large and important country. By 1900 the United States was a great *world power*.

yacht (yot) A boat used for pleasure.

Learning Strategies

The lesson plans for the Student Book activities present and practice the following learning strategies. For further discussion of these strategies, please refer to the Teacher's Guide.

Student Book pages

Metacognitive Strategies

Advance Organization
Previewing the main ideas and concepts of the material to be learned, often by skimming the text for the organizing principle.

12, 13, 15, 16, 18, 20–21, 22–23, 32–35, 42–43, 46–49, 52, 54–55, 61, 68, 72–73, 76–80, 82–83, 85–88, 92–101.

Advance Preparation
Rehearsing the language needed for an oral or written task.

36–39, 44–45, 62–64, 74–75, 102–105, 106–107.

Organizational Planning
Planning the parts, sequence, and main ideas to be expressed orally or in writing.

36–39, 62–64, 70–71, 102–105.

Selective Attention
Attending to or scanning key words, phrases, linguistic markers, sentences, or types of information.

15, 17–19, 22–23, 24–27, 30–33, 36–43, 48–60, 62–73, 78–91, 96–105.

Self-Evaluation
Judging how well one has accomplished a learning activity after it has been completed.

14, 16, 19, 26, 28–29, 32–41, 44–45, 50–51, 53–71, 74–75, 78–81, 85–87, 89, 92–95, 98–107.

Cognitive Strategies

Contextualization
Placing a word or phrase in a meaningful sentence or category.

14, 27, 48–49, 50–51, 74–75, 85–87.

Elaboration
Relating new information to what is already known.

17, 24–25, 32–33, 36–39, 42–45, 50–51, 61, 66–67, 70–75, 84, 90–91, 96–97, 106–107.

Grouping
Classifying words, terminology, or concepts according to their attributes.

14, 40–41, 42–43, 70–71, 96–97.

Imagery
Using visual images (either mental or actual) to understand and remember new information.

13, 15, 17–26, 28–31, 34–52, 56–59, 62–64, 72–73, 77–79, 81, 84, 90–91, 94–97, 106–107.

Student Book pages

Inferencing
Using information in the text to guess meanings of new items, predict outcomes, or complete missing parts.

13–25, 27–45, 47–61, 65–75, 77–107.

Note-taking
Writing down key words and concepts in abbreviated form during a listening or reading activity.

22–26, 36–41, 44–45, 48–49, 56–57, 60, 62–64, 68–71, 74–75, 82–83, 85–89, 92–95, 98–107.

Resourcing
Using reference materials such as dictionaries, encyclopedias, or textbooks.

14, 17, 20–21, 24–25, 27, 30–41, 48–49, 54–55, 62–64, 80, 84–87, 89, 92–95.

Summarizing
Making a mental or written summary of information gained through listening or reading.

15, 20–23, 26, 28–39, 42–43, 52–60, 66–68, 72–73, 78–80, 88–89, 94–97, 102–103.

Transfer
Using what is already known to facilitate a learning task.

12–14, 22–25, 27, 34–35, 40–41, 44–51, 58–59, 65–67, 69–80, 82–88, 90–93, 98–101, 106–107.

Social Affective Strategies

Cooperation
Working together with peers to solve a problem, pool information, check a learning task, or get feedback on oral or written performance.

14, 16–23, 26–45, 48–75, 78–107.

Questioning for Clarification
Eliciting from a teacher or peer additional explanation, rephrasing, or examples.

13, 15, 18, 20–21, 24–25, 34–39, 42–43, 47–49, 53, 56–57, 62–68, 77, 80, 84–88, 92–93, 96–97, 102–105.

Academic Skills

This index lists academic skills emphasized in the Student Book activities. Additional practice in these skills is often provided in preparatory and follow-up activities in the Teacher's Guide lesson plans.

Listening and Speaking Skills

Student Book pages

Discussion issues, supporting opinions	19, 22, 29, 33, 45, 50, 51, 54, 61, 67, 73, 75, 82, 85, 91, 97, 105, 107
Preparing and giving oral presentations	37, 45, 63, 75, 105, 107
Understanding oral presentations	23, 37, 54, 60, 64, 89, 105

Reading Comprehension Skills

Comparing and contrasting	19, 31, 33, 49, 54, 71, 73, 81, 83, 97, 105
Determining meaning through context	33, 51, 54, 61, 67, 87
Drawing conclusions and inferences, making generalizations	16, 24, 40, 44, 45, 49, 52, 57, 61, 65, 67, 71, 73, 74, 75, 84, 91, 97, 105, 106, 107
Incorporating information from maps, graphs	15, 16, 18, 24, 25, 43, 44, 57, 59, 73, 81, 84, 91
Making predictions	22, 67, 82, 98
Recalling details	16, 29, 40, 44, 49, 51, 52, 55, 61, 68, 71, 73, 74, 75, 79, 82, 83, 87, 89, 91, 93, 106, 107
Recognizing or inferring main idea	16, 19, 27, 36, 49, 53, 54, 55, 62, 64, 65, 68, 71, 74, 75, 79, 83, 87, 89, 91, 92, 93, 100, 102, 105, 106, 107
Recognizing cause and effect	29, 43, 67, 82, 83, 91, 97, 107
Recognizing same information phrased differently	16, 29, 40, 44, 69, 71, 97
Relating one's own experiences to the material	17, 22, 24, 33, 43, 45, 50, 67, 73, 75, 82, 85, 88, 91, 97, 101–105, 107
Scanning for specific information	15, 25, 36, 39, 40, 41, 43, 44, 51, 52, 62, 79, 83, 87, 93, 97, 98, 106
Skimming for an overview	20, 98
Synthesizing and elaborating, making judgments	19, 22, 29, 33, 43, 45, 51, 54, 55, 57, 61, 65, 67, 68, 73, 75, 82, 84, 91, 97, 102, 107

Map Skills

Charting locations and routes on a map	15, 39, 45, 52, 57, 79
Comparing two maps	13, 15, 17, 18, 24, 3 0, 41, 45, 84, 91
Locating places on a map	15, 17, 18, 24, 30, 39, 41, 52, 57, 59, 81, 84, 91
Understanding cardinal (compass) directions	15, 18, 31, 44, 52, 57, 59, 73, 91
Using map key, scale of miles, latitude lines	15, 17, 31, 39, 41, 52, 57, 59, 73, 79, 81

Study Skills

Classifying	15, 18, 30, 43, 57, 73, 83, 84, 87, 91, 97
Following directions	15, 20, 36, 52, 54, 62, 101–102
Interpreting and making data charts, bar graphs, pie graphs, time lines	25, 42–43, 49, 59, 81, 92, 93, 96–97, 101
Making study charts, writing study questions	23, 25, 41, 83, 85, 93, 100, 102
Taking notes from oral presentations	23, 38, 60, 64, 89, 105
Taking notes from reading selections	36, 41, 62, 68, 79, 83, 100
Using a dictionary or glossary	14, 27, 33, 34, 48, 69, 78
Using an encyclopedia, almanac, reference books	25, 31, 36, 62, 87, 93

Writing Skills

Organizing and writing a report	36, 55, 62, 93, 102–104
Summarizing	33, 53, 55, 61, 62, 68, 75, 79, 83, 87, 93, 102–104
Transforming graphic information into sentences	23, 31, 49
Writing complete sentences	14, 27, 75, 107
Writing paragraphs	23, 31, 53, 68